Ultimate Acceptance
The last patrol

By William Barnes

Copyright

© June 2012 by Sandhills Management Consultancy Limited.

All rights reserved. No part of this document may be reproduced or transmitted in any form or by any means, electronic, mechanical, photocopying, recording, or otherwise, without prior written permission of Sandhills Management Consultancy Limited.

Author's note

In writing this book I have tried to recreate events, locales and conversations from my memories of them. In order to maintain their anonymity in some instances I have changed the names of individuals and places, I may also have changed some identifying characteristics and details such as physical properties.

Version 1.1 12 November 2012

Contents

Ultimate Acceptance 0
Copyright 1
Chapter 1 4
   Warminster 1981 4
Chapter 2 10
   Hereford April 1982 10
Chapter 3 24
   Hereford May 1982 24
Chapter 4 41
   COBRA Whitehall London May 1982 41
Chapter 5 46
   Ascension Island May 1982 46
Chapter 6 53
   South Atlantic May 1982 53
Chapter 7 70
   HMS Hermes May 1982 70
Chapter 8 81
   Leave 1980 81
Chapter 9 96
   HMS Invincible May 1982 96

Chapter 10	109
Central America 1981	109
Chapter 11	112
Oman 1981	112
Chapter 12	117
Insertion May 1982	117
Chapter 13	123
Insertion	123
Chapter 14	133
Chile	133
Chapter 15	149
Recovery	149
Chapter 16	171
Pickup	171
Chapter 17	183
Epilogue 30 years later	183
Appendix	189
Timeline	190

Chapter 1

Warminster 1981

The Colonel stood up to address the assembled Junior Division of Staff College course and introduce the main speaker. The topic for the afternoon discussion was Special Forces Operations and the main presentation would be given by the Director himself. The course was a mixed group of about 60 officers with the rank of Captain or equivalent, both male and female, mainly from across the Army. They were all in their late 20s to early 30s. Attending the course was a prerequisite to further promotion in their chosen profession and so most attendees took the whole business very seriously.

"The man I am about to present to you needs no introduction, he is one of the most experienced soldiers in the British Army participating in many campaigns, including Korea, Aden, Borneo and Oman. He has served with distinction with the SAS as Troop Commander, Squadron Commander and CO. He holds the MC for his actions in Borneo and the DSO for his leadership in Oman. He is now the Director of Special Forces Operations."

The Colonel continued, "We know you are an extremely busy man Brigadier and are most grateful to you for taking the time to come and address the course."

The Brigadier stood up to begin his presentation. It was as to be expected, most impressive, as a speaker he was highly eloquent and he covered a brief history of SAS operations starting from the Long Range Patrol Group in North Africa, through to Malaya, Aden, Borneo, Oman, and then to counter terrorist operations in Northern Ireland and UK. The audience were clearly captivated. He covered the principles of how the SAS would interact with the government and police in counter terrorist operations. Where SAS soldiers were deployed he stressed the strategic nature of such operations and the way in which Governments should expect to use Special Forces.

To one of the members of the assembled audience, Jim, much of what was said was not really new as he had heard the content a number of times previously. That was not to say he did not find it interesting and in many ways an excellent presentation, it was always good to learn from a master. Jim also felt very proud to be more directly associated than most of the assembled company with some of the topics under review, as he had been an SAS Troop commander for almost 2 years. Lord knows it had been hard enough to get into the Regiment and as everyone was told when they were first given the Who Dares Wins badge it was even harder to keep it.

Sitting near to him was a young Royal Marine helicopter pilot who also felt some affinity, having previously flown Special Forces operations he too had more in common with the subject matter than most.

During subsequent questions the Brigadier gave a surprisingly personal insight. He emphasised that there would be some times when it would be necessary for them all to take what he described as "hard decisions." Jim who was listening carefully thought, "Hard decisions, surely everyone in the room takes them from time to time?"

The Brigadier continued. He went on to describe, in outline only, a situation when as a young troop commander he had found it necessary to pull his loaded 9mm pistol, put it to the head of one of the team under his command and threaten to kill him. Whilst not giving the detailed circumstances, in essence there had been a disagreement over the level to which any support for the members of the team doing the job might or might not override the mission. It was clear to Jim that when it came to the crunch the Brigadier was saying that whilst loyalty to the team was always important it should never be allowed to cloud the judgement of any commander when or if it threatens the mission.

The Brigadier concluded his presentation and there was polite applause from the audience. The Colonel led the Brigadier away. The assembled officers quickly dispersed to grab a quick cup of tea before completing their preparatory work for the following day. Jim was in a bit of a rush because he wanted to squeeze in a quick run before dinner with a couple of the others, do his work and still have time for the regulatory couple of beers in the mess afterwards.

He quickly changed into his running kit and met the others who were also going on the run. One of the runners was a WRAC Captain, Kate, she was in his syndicate and he found her great company. Not least of which she was good looking, extremely fit and had recently taken to getting changed into running kit in his room, as she lived off site. The whole business had become a little distracting and Jim was forced to admit to himself that at times it was hard to concentrate on the course!

During the run over the surrounding Warminster hills when his gaze wasn't transfixed on Kate tight shorts he tried to reflect a little on what "hard decisions" might really mean. Over the past 18 months he had become very close to the troop he commanded. They had been asked to perform some difficult and sometimes dangerous tasks. Everyone had without exception approached the tasks in a positive spirit and always with a degree of humour despite the adversity; he found it quite hard therefore to imagine circumstances where he would be totally at loggerheads with the team. He knew within the troop that there was an unwritten and unstated rule at least in public, that whatever the nature of the task you took care of your own people first. Sure knowing that your team were resourceful helped and they would always one way or another to complete the mission, but not the other way round. Better to plan to all go together or all succeed together rather than any other way. In this sense loyalty to the team when taken to the extreme almost overrode the mission, or did it? Jim realised that this was probably not an acceptable premise and pondered whether having doubts and maybe even asking himself such questions meant that he was probably not cut out to be a senior officer. Anyway dispelling any such thoughts and forcing the pace a little, he reflected that there were far more immediate and stressful things ahead. Kate getting showered and then changed in his room for one!

Later on that evening after dinner and preparation Jim was in the bar with a team of cohorts including the young helicopter pilot Jeff. Over a few pints they discussed the events of the day. Jim was continually getting banter about his relationship or otherwise with Kate. He smiled and pushed the comments to one side and insisted they were just good friends, Jim brought up the Brigadier's comments regarding hard decisions. Conventional wisdom seemed to be that the greater good should always prevail although interestingly the two with some Special Forces experience seemed less sure and believed there were elements of grey. They all agreed that they would rather not be put into such a situation, whilst loyalty was in general the preferred option circumstances could arise when it might be necessary to test this to the limit.

Several pints later and the world seemed a much jollier place and the conversation had quickly moved on to rugby and then back to fit women on the course. Both topics suited Jim just fine and ordering another round he moved the more difficult questions to the back of his mind.

Chapter 2

Hereford April 1982

For the past weeks the Squadron had been in preparation for war. The level of activity was intense. Since the outbreak of hostilities Jim and the squadron had all been involved in a seemingly endless series of day and night exercises, sometimes involving parachuting on land and sea, endurance marching, range work, working with explosives, and patrol and ambush drills. This in itself was hardly surprising given what was going on 8,000 miles away and so initially there had been a real buzz of excitement; under normal circumstances everyone in the Squadron would to a man, have looked forward with eager anticipation for their orders to deploy. When D and G squadrons had deployed with the Task Force earlier there was a genuine sense of having missed out on the excitement.

The whole thing had begun with a hastily arranged briefing in B Squadron lines early on Sunday 4 April. The Squadron had been called in to be told by the OC that the training in Canada planned for the next month had been cancelled and that as a result of the Argentinian invasion of the Falklands on 2 April 1982, B Squadron was on standby for deployment. There was a map of South America on the briefing board, but no further details were available and the OC explained that they would be undergoing some intensive training until their mission became clear.

However as the days wore on and the training became more and focused, certain elements of it became slightly disturbing, some might say almost alarming. It had all started with a briefing for a 'raid on Entebbe' style of operation. To start with this was greeted with enthusiasm. It was initially described by the Operations Officer as the Squadron simply rehearsing for a number of possible deployment options. This raid involved the drills associated with two C130 aircraft flying low level, supposed below the ground radar and then landing on the enemy airfield. Although not explicitly mentioned everyone knew unofficially that the eventual targets would likely be one of two principal airfields in the Southern Argentinian mainland and Tierra del Fuego, Rio Gallegos and Rio Grande respectively. It was supposed that the Super Etendard aircraft were operating with Exocets against the task force from these airfields.

The two assigned C130 aircraft from RAF Lyneham contained the whole of Jim's Squadron together with mobility troop vehicles, land rovers with rear mounted machine guns. Once the C130s had successfully landed on the airfield the Squadron mission was to destroy any enemy aircraft, the control tower and infrastructure, kill pilots and ground support staff and generally create mayhem.

So here they all were back in Hereford signing out their weapons from the armoury for another night time jaunt, this time to practice a hit on an RAF airfield off the North

East Coast of Scotland. It was about ten minutes to midnight on a cold and frosty early April night.

"Evening Kev," Jim said. He could see his breath in the cold air.

"Evening Boss, looking forward to the briefing?"

Kev his troop SSgt waited for Jim to catch up, he managed a smile. "You know I really can't get my head around this option and why the fuck they think it can be a success. Surely someone will come to their senses?"

Jim nodded, "All seems way out of our control, no one is interested in what we think or how we might approach the problem some alternative way, at least that's the way it feels" he said it with a touch of resignation, adding "Don't you just love it, this low level flying really agrees with me. The smell of petrol and puke, I just can't wait."

"This exercise," said Kev, "I think it's more about finding out whether the powers that be think that low level flying can come in under the radar, rather than what we might or might not be able to do on the ground."

"Suspect you are right, do you think they will want to tell us the results?" said Jim.

"We are just pawns Boss," said Kev.

"Not such a good analogy, I'd rather not think that we are not that expendable," Jim replied.

"We are being driven by some desperate men, Boss" Jim managed to smile, Kev had some great expressions.

One of his theories was that most cock ups were drink related. Someone taking their eye off the ball because either they were suffering from too much or were so keen to look out for the next opportunity that they missed the main point. Jim wasn't sure he totally agreed but was forced to admit that Kev certainly had a point. Take a recent job; they had been given an advisory task which had meant an early flight to Portugal. The driver taking them to the airport was late; they subsequently discovered he had been out on the town. They had been caught in rush hour traffic, missed the flight which had caused a bit of a stir all the way through the system to the Military Attaché waiting at the airport to meet the flight they had missed. All a bit embarrassing and Kev had been keen to remind Jim that the root cause had been drink.

They both collected their weapons from the armoury, M16 rifles and for backup Browning 9mm pistols. Then they headed into the Squadron Lines for the OCs briefing where the rest of the Squadron were gathering.

20 minutes later Jim, Kev and the others were getting into the back of 4 tonners heading off for RAF Lyneham. Over the past couple of years Jim and his team had got so used to the route from Hereford to Lyneham, they could practically describe it blindfolded. It was usually the beginning or end of some adventure. The shortcut

round Birdlip near Gloucester stuck particularly in his mind and if there was time the boys always appreciated a quick visit to the burger stand; even if it was conveniently situated at the back of the public toilets in the Cirencester car park. Not that there was any prospect of a bacon sandwich for the guys tonight, this was far too serious.

Anyway as Kev wisely pointed out when discussing the matter with Snapper, "Just as well eh Snapper, nay time for any burgers, if we stopped we'd only being seeing them all again later in the back of the C130. Mark my words; if it's anything like the last one at least half the Squadron will be sick. Don't forget lads it might well make the back of the C130 a little slippery, so you'll need to take care when running out of the back!"

"Thanks Kev, you've really helped us along, I feel better already." Jim replied.

For the past few days Jim had been thinking about attempting the operation for real. Apart from the odd joke he hadn't said anything but he felt slightly concerned about the chances of ever reaching the objective intact. Now he was feeling queasy with the prospect of another bout of air sickness. Fucking great, life doesn't get much better! He reflected.

Jim had a great deal of respect for Kev. He had worked closely with him in Oman, Northern Ireland and on the UK anti-terrorist team. Never one for the bull at the gate approach, Kev considered his options carefully. He had originally joined the regiment from the Paras and having passed selection at the age of 21, he now had a good 16 years of operational experience in the regiment under his belt. He had been on SAS operations in Borneo, Oman, Northern Ireland and most recently at the Iranian Embassy. When Jim first joined the troop he observed the others in the troop looked to Kev, it was clear they respected his judgement.

Over the past 2 years Jim had grown close to Kev and considered him as a good friend. Recently they had been sent on a reconnaissance mission for an anti-terrorist training team job in Portugal. Whist the work had been serious they had a good time. Jim managed to smile, he was thinking about their arrival. After missing the plane they had been taken to a very expensive hotel in Lisbon by the Portuguese liaison officer. There was some confusion over whether they would need to pay the bill from their expenses allowance or whether the tab would be picked up by the local team. Knowing that any shortfall would need to be met by themselves and both being broke they decided to play it safe. They had calculated they could just about pay the bill and the rest of the trip from their allowance if they ate cheaply out of the hotel and only drank in the cheaper bars. So having had omelettes every night they were completely gutted to find at the end of the trip the hotel expenses were paid locally.

As the roads were quiet the journey to Lyneham took just over an hour. During the trip it was decidedly chilly so they were glad to dismount with their equipment on the runway, right next to the two C130s. The four 'pink panther' land rovers had already arrived separately as they were being driven directly by Mobility troop. These were now in the process of being loaded onto the planes first, two per aircraft.

The idea of the assault was fairly straightforward; using the old SAS principle of speed, aggression and surprise the land rovers would head off for the control tower seeking to destroy it, followed by destruction or at least mutilation of the hangars, ground staff and support infrastructure and anything else that got in the way. The other two troops would take care of securing the C130s, any enemy aircraft and hopefully the ground defence forces too. The plan was for a team to use explosive timing devices set on a short fuse and for the rest to provide cover against enemy forces guarding the airfield. The teams would pull back to the C130s immediately prior to the short fuse explosive charges going off. In the resulting mayhem the C130s would attempt to take off so that the Squadron would be able to escape.

In addition to the land rovers approximately 25 men were assigned to each aircraft. Initially everything went fine but after about 30 minutes it was fairly obvious that they were starting to fly low level as there was a significant level of turbulence. This combined with the strong smell of petrol from the vehicles was too much for many of the troop, there were quite a few white faces and the sick bags soon began to appear.

When Jim started parachuting at Brize Norton an old paratrooper instructor had said "Boss, sometimes when the turbulence is bad it gets absolutely heaving on the plane, you'll be trying to stand up with your container sweating bullets, slipping on the puke and in the end you will be so glad to jump out you will not give a fuck whether you have a chute."

Jim hadn't believed him at the time although subsequently there were several times when those words had been proven to be well, almost true. This time there was no parachutes but the petrol and turbulence were definitely doing their best to make up for the disappointment. Fight it he thought, you can always throw up later on the airfield when no one is looking.

They were given the 10 minute warning to the target by the loadmaster so everyone began to take up their dismounting positions. The drivers and crew ready in their vehicles. The ground assault teams were lined up around the vehicles, with their M16 rifles in one hand and unfortunately for many a sick bag in the other. Jim was standing next to the driver of the first land rover, Don who paused in mid-sentence to carefully use his sick bag.

When he had finished he asked Jim, "How you feeling Boss, you look pretty green?"

"Thanks Don have to say that I have felt better, but I reckon I can make it until we get off the fucking plane."

"Attack the enemy with a sea of puke, that'll do the job." Don tried to laugh.

At the same moment Jim finally unable to supress it any longer gave an involuntary heave, quick as a flash Don moved the bag and caught what was heading straight onto the soldier in front.

Jim was amazed and grateful. So would the person in front be if they had known how close, he later reflected.

"All about teamwork Boss," Don grinned managing a wink despite adversity.

Everyone watched the lights. Eventually after what seemed to be an age the red light showed up, this was their warning for 2 minutes to landing. The engines on the land rovers were started.

Jim, now feeling a little better was trying hard to focus on the task in hand, he was certain that the adrenalin would see him through.

The plane bumped slightly as it landed and quickly taxied into position. Almost immediately the back lowered and just before it was completely down the land rovers roared off into the darkness. Jim, Kev and the rest of his team ran out of the back trying to locate their targets. In front of him Jim could see the rest of the Squadron pouring out of the back of the second C130.

"Fuck, its cold" Jim ran off into the falling snow, "definitely not spring in Scotland yet" he thought.

During the briefing they had been told that assuming the landings went as planned their targets would be approximately 200 metres expected to be at 3 o'clock from the rear of the C130 landing position. Slightly unreal perhaps but this was an exercise.

For real there would likely be many other factors to consider. In this exercise no meaningful resistance would be encountered, for real you would probably not know where the aircraft were located and there would probably be someone shooting at you.

Despite waves of nausea Jim and the others moved rapidly through the snow and located the 3 target aircraft; whilst Jim staked out the area with one team Kev led the team planting the explosives.

Within 6 minutes Jim reported back on the radio to the Squadron HQ that their task was complete and they were immediately ordered back to the plane. As they arrived back the land rovers were already loading back onto the aircraft. The C130 engines had remained on during the operation and the planes had turned and were starting to move by the time Jim and his 11 men made it back on board. The tailgate raised and everyone collapsed against the fuselage.

The trip back passed fairly uneventfully and after the excitement Jim managed about an hour's kip. More kip followed in the back of the 4 tonner even if it was a bit uncomfortable, then the sickness having passed there was time to grab a quick tea and bacon sandwich before the OCs debrief.

During the wash up back at Hereford the OC commented that overall he thought the execution had been good. No comments were made about how easily or otherwise it had been to detect the C130s. There was probably a general feeling of disquiet. Although everyone had initially found the idea quite exciting, to Jim and many of his colleagues there were a number of unanswered questions.

Maybe you could get away with this type of raid in a true Third World scenario but would this enemy really be unprepared, ill equipped or so stupid as to allow 2 unidentified aircraft to land on an enemy military airbase in the middle of a war zone, especially on their home soil?

Jim supposed not, his Troop SSgt Kev definitely thought not and between the naps on the way back the whole thing had been a hot topic of conversation amongst the various teams within the Squadron.

One of the NCOs from another troop asked what would happen if we were picked up on enemy radar, how likely would it be that we would be able to land? The OC had simply answered that the master plan was to ensure that there would be a Spanish speaker on board to confuse the enemy ground crew giving them sufficient time and the opportunity to land.

Another question followed, "what happens if we land and the escape aircraft get damaged or destroyed?" The OC had explained that there was an exfiltration plan, a good word essentially dispersal and then head west about 60 km to the Chilean border. This was also been greeted with silence. Everyone had probably already worked that out for themselves. Strangely there were no more questions after this.

After the debriefing and over another mug of tea, Jim discussed it further with Kev and his troop NCOs.

"I think the Spanish speaker idea is a bit tenuous Kev," he had said.

"Most stupid fucking idea I've ever heard, Boss, more likely we'll go up in a fireball before we ever land. You can bet your arse that the clown who is dreaming this lot up will not be in the back of the C130 participating," was the somewhat terse reply.

Kev continued, "So what happens to us if we ever did land? If the planes get damaged in the shoot-out we'll be stuffed anyway and about 30 km from the Chilean border. It feels like they want to write off a fucking squadron to prove a point."

Jim felt Kev was right too but decided it was best to keep quiet, which to be fair was becoming increasingly difficult. He noted for balance that this wasn't a unanimous point of view. There were still a couple of the lads who were saying bring it on, Jim wasn't really sure whether they were being serious, fair play though he thought, everyone is entitled to their opinion. Lofty a tough ex RE soldier was the most vociferous, "…don't give a fuck Boss let's just do it." However the general consensus in the troop and probably the squadron was all things considered that this was still a pretty shitty option. The chances of such a mission succeeding were clearly very low and perhaps more to the point pretty much completely outside of the control of the main participants. The obvious fear was that more than likely they would all be shot down before they ever would be able to reach the target and do anything to help the war effort.

Perhaps more disturbing to Jim was that even with the low probability of success, and most likely this would already been evaluated more formally as part of the planning, the senior officers were still prepared to risk an entire squadron in the event that despite all adversity they could still pull something off.

Privately Jim believed his Squadron Commander (OC) also didn't believe the way of executing mission they were training for was viable. He did understand that in public at least the OC could not be very open in his views, especially if he wanted to keep his job. There being a fine dividing line between open dissent, making yourself very unpopular and remaining in place to perhaps at least exerting some moderating influence on those wanting the mission to go ahead.

The OC had never discussed the mission with Jim and it was clear the whole thing was being driven very much top down. Jim felt that it would have been good to have been asked for his opinion, to at least have discussed options openly with the other officers and senior NCOs in the Squadron; this would have been quite normal SAS practice in most theatres. In this instance Jim could only assume there was such pressure from above that questioning the viability of the mission was a complete no go area.

Chapter 3

Hereford May 1982

0500hrs with thin grey cloud covering the sky over Hereford, despite it being early May there was a distinct chill in the air. The patrol was loading their equipment into the back of the 4 Tonner. Not so much of the usual banter thought Jim. The mood amongst the men in the patrol seemed rather bleak perhaps also reflecting the level of difficulty and uncertainty surrounding their mission. If he had been put on a rack at that moment he would have been forced to admit that perhaps for the first time, in a fairly brief but quite eventful military career, he too had some serious misgivings.

"Morning Len", said Jim.

The SSM had turned up to see them off; he was a great guy, highly experienced with a good sense of humour. Normally when the chips were down everyone could rely on some good honest black humour to raise their spirits, especially from Len. On this occasion whilst it was always good to see him it didn't help with the sense of gloomy resignation.

"Morning Jim, everything OK?"

"Just about ready to go now, I think", Jim replied.

"Listen Jim, I know this is a bit sticky, remember to take it steady, move slowly at first and have a good look around before you do anything".

Trying to make light of a difficult situation the SSM added with a wry smile, "Besides you guys really are the lucky ones, think of the rest of us stuck inside the C130 while the missiles are raining down!"

Jim did see the funny side, even tried to smile, but somehow there was always a comfort in being with the rest of the Squadron, no matter what was put in front of them. The isolation of this job was helping towards the general malaise.

Looking back over the past month they had certainly trained hard for this moment. Somehow though he did not feel as energetic or enthusiastic and he should and this also made him feel even slightly guilty. The standing joke amongst the boys was that none of the deskbound team who had dreamt the plans and subsequent training exercises over the past few weeks would be taking part in the real thing.

In most Special Forces actions Jim felt that those taking part at least had more say in the viability and planning of options, the method of entry or execution, than in the normal Army, but not so here. He and his patrol and indeed even the whole Squadron were more or less at mushroom level, being moved around like pawns by senior officers and the politicians.

He had said his goodbyes to family and close friends at home and on the phone earlier, being somewhat circumspect about his forthcoming deployment, saying only that at long last he had been requested to join up with the Task Force. He had tried to sound enthusiastic to his family as he always had on previous such occasions. They knew how much he loved his job. However this one felt a bit different. Those closest to him had sensed his mood was different but other that wishing him luck and a safe and speedy return had wisely decided not to comment further. He had been barely at home for the past month anyway. The previous night with such dark thoughts slowly eating away at his sanity he had slept only fitfully. As a result Jim felt surprisingly weary while loading his Bergen into the back of the 4 tonner. He shook hands with the SSM saying a quick farewell.

"See you on the airfield, we will be there before you," he joked. He then climbed into the back with the rest of the Patrol and they departed for RAF Brize Norton. They were all dressed in civvies, the plan being to reunite them with their uniform and equipment at a later stage.

Yesterday afternoon they had even been given patrol orders by no less a person that the SAS Brigadier himself. Right up to this point Jim felt almost certain that somewhere along the line of command a degree of common sense would prevail. In a rare moment of humour earlier the previous day Snapper one of his troop, had joked that he had heard on the news that the various UN peace initiatives appeared to be bearing fruit. Given this we might not actually get deployed or arrive too late. They had all laughed, most unusual for this lot ever to want a peaceful outcome to any scrap thought Jim.

Also it was quite an odd scenario for an SAS patrol to be briefed by the SAS Director in person at least it seemed so to Jim. Normally Jim supposed that this would have been deemed quite an honour, however in this situation it just seemed to add, perhaps quite unnecessarily, to the pressure and what had become a huge level of in Jim's opinion quite possibly misplaced expectation. Normally there were Squadron Commanders and Operations Officers all vying for the role, all wanting to be part of the action.

The patrol had been shut away for the previous 2 days to plan. Normally an essential part of any mission and so on the face of it seemed like a good idea; except that there was really very little information to plan with. The weather had been warm and sunny outside and being stuck inside a hot and smelly room for all this time with nothing much tangible to play with didn't seem to make much sense to any of them. They were all bored of waiting for something to happen. The supplied maps appeared to have been cut out of a 1930's school atlas and there were a small number of older aerial photographs of the target that rumour had it had been obtained from personal contacts with American special forces. The team had asked if there was any more detailed or up to date information and complained to the Operation support team about the lack of quality intelligence but all to no avail.

Given the absence of topological detail on any available map it was almost impossible to relate the photo to it. There were just a few lines showing the coastline and some names like 'Estancia Cameron' on white paper. Nothing was shown to indicate the location of airstrips or centres of population. The location of the target was just a name on the map. No details of the ground surrounding it were to be seen. To the west there was a comment "relief not believed to be above 10,000 feet".

No intelligence existed or at least had been made available about the deployment or strength of enemy forces around the target locations, nor across the whole of the area between the sea to the East and the border to the West. There was no information on the location of Super Etendard aircraft, pilots or ground crew. What was the border like? Was it just an imaginary line in open country or was it guarded and were there mines and obstacles?

Jim was almost certain that the enemy would be on a war footing and from what he had gleaned they had reasonably sophisticated air defences so any helicopter or C130 insertion would need to take this into account.

To the team the only sensible conclusion to be drawn therefore, given the uncertainty was that moving slowly across the border overland from Chile in the west would certainly constitute the least risk option. It gave the patrol the opportunity to fill in some of the gaps as they probed slowly eastwards towards the target. Also moving in such a way would minimise the risks of compromising the patrol and so in the longer term stood the best chance of success.

Jim expressed this view to the operations staff on a number of occasions, it was certainly not popular. The feeling was it required a level of political cooperation with Chile that was at least yet not in place and so any operation of this nature would take more time to execute. Time was fast running out. The planner's favoured option therefore appeared to be entry by sea from the east reducing the distance to the target airfield. Pointless arguing further thought Jim, realizing he if he made himself too unpopular by expressing doubts he would run the risk of getting the chop.

The nature of the mission was also unclear. Originally the intention had been to perform reconnaissance to determine the location of enemy aircraft and understand the strength of enemy forces protecting them. This intelligence would be used by the rest of the Squadron to seek and destroy enemy aircraft and supporting teams or equipment in a second stage. At the last minute however it had been decided to merge 2 patrols moving from 4 to 8 men and to order them to take a quantity of explosives and timing devices. Given limitations of Bergen capacity and weight this meant ditching some other food and other equipment. As a result the patrol was now, in Jim's opinion, ill equipped for a longer term reconnaissance mission. It would need to be an in and out job.

The patrol listened carefully to the Brigadier's briefing. Despite the gravity of the situation Jim found it hard to concentrate, it all seemed slightly surreal.

"Congratulations on passing your staff college exams Jim" the Brigadier opened up quietly with a personal remark.

Jim had completely forgotten the results had been available today, under different circumstances he would have been very pleased. He might well have had a few beers that evening to celebrate, no such luck today. "Thank you, sir" Jim said, trying to sound enthusiastic. In part, wondering whether he would ever be able to reap the rewards of such success.

Formalities over and looking round the briefing room trying to catch everyone's eye the Brigadier continued. "These are your orders. You all no doubt understand the position regarding the fragility of the task force position and what might happen should we lose one of the carriers." Everyone nodded.

He continued, "Your mission is to identify the location of the enemy aircraft and destroy them."

So it now looks like we are definitely not just on a reconnaissance mission then thought Jim.

The Brigadier described the route that the patrol would take to join up with the task force.

"You will leave here at 0500hrs tomorrow, be taken to RAF Brize Norton where you will fly by VC10 to Ascension Island via Dakar where your plane will refuel"

A brief pause, Jim looked around he could see what the boys were thinking. Likely to be along the lines of come on that's the holiday bit of the trip over, what happens next? Jim tried to recall his geography, Dakar on the west coast of Africa, yes that's about it.

The Brigadier continued, "Your equipment will be transported separately to Ascension Island and you will collect it when you arrive. Travel to Ascension Island will be in civilian clothes and you will change into uniform for the remainder of the mission."

Seeming not to pause for breath the Brigadier outlined the next stage.

"From Ascension Island you will fly by C130 which has been specially equipped with long range fuel tanks to a position near a RNFA vessel. You will then parachute into the sea with your equipment. I'm advised you will need wet suits, the water is quite cold, so you will need to pack your equipment as waterproof as possible."

Still no reaction from the team, all quiet. Fuck, I wonder what the South Atlantic feels like at this time of year; Jim suspected everyone else was thinking the same.

"You will be picked up from the sea, taken on-board, and then collected by sea king helicopter and taken onto a carrier, likely to be HMS Invincible."

At this point the scale of the operation hit Jim. Shit! All this and we still haven't even got anywhere near the fucking target.

The Brigadier paused a little looking for reaction around the room, seeing none he went on.

"There are a number of possibilities on how we get you to the target location. Option 1 is we use a sea king helicopter. There are several difficulties with this approach, not least of which the range of the helicopter means it can only be a one way trip. Effectively this means writing off a valuable and scarce asset. You would fly in at wave height to avoid detection by enemy radar"

No reaction from the patrol, perhaps they were feeling stunned. Jim's immediate thoughts were why would you waste a helicopter and aircrew on an option with such limited chance of success? Then given the lack of detail on the ground, helicopters make a fair bit of noise so we certainly don't want to wind up in the wrong place attracting lots of unwelcome attention!

"Moving on to option 2 then", said the Brigadier.

Option 2 is that we transfer you from HMS Invincible or other suitable task force vessel to a submarine or a fast patrol boat, from where you will move into a position just off the east coast and be taken by inflatable into the mainland."

Both of these have the potential to drop us right into the shit, always assuming we get there, thought Jim, still trying hard not to reveal any emotion. We hit the beach and what then? What about some consideration of option 3? We the people doing the job all agreed that given the uncertainty it would be a better option to infiltrate across the border from the west. There was no mention of option 3, definitely no subtlety here, effectively a full frontal assault into the unknown. Great, 8,000 miles to all get wet and then we get dumped on some god forsaken beach and are left to get on with it. Surprisingly the latter part of this thought was the most appealing thing that had happened for some weeks.

Back to reality, the brigadier continued with a final flourish, "You will receive further orders when you arrive in Ascension Island, so some of the details regarding insertion may change. After a brief stopover you will be loaded with your equipment onto specially converted C130. This will need to be refuelled in flight from Ascension Island to the DZ. The run in may vary as there is a lot of enemy air activity. When over the DZ the aircrew will determine whether weather conditions are suitable for the drop. If not it may be necessary to return to Ascension and try again another day."

The briefing entered the final stages, as suspected there would be satellite communication back to the UK, which would be the responsibility of Nick the signals specialist.

Jim's team had worked with the satellite communications devices before whilst working with the US Delta team and he knew that these had been acquired as a result of the close relationships that existed at a personal level with their American Special Forces counterparts. The satellite communication set, whilst still bulky was claimed to be completely secure, enabling rapid communications at specified period of the day when the satellite was overhead. No need to waste time on one time pad encryption and Morse code transmission when using these babies. This it was planned would enable the patrol to keep in close touch with HQ and SAS Directorate throughout the mission.

Of course despite the obvious advantages there was now the risk that instead of the patrol commander running the mission on the ground there would be lots of help from 8,000 miles away. As ever a bit of a mixed blessing, plenty of scope for some meddling then, you are never alone with the latest Satellite communications. Jim had to remind himself to concentrate, being slightly cynical he thought was always rather healthy but he was starting to take it to an art form.

The status of the operation didn't seem that clear either when they got to the bit on actions on compromise. If they heaven forbid, were captured would they be treated as soldiers or spies, would the Government would officially deny the whole operation? Surely not, Jim thought, he was just being paranoid.

Obviously the success or otherwise of the mission depended upon remaining undetected. The Brigadier had included a statement on actions if compromised.

"You may wish to consider carefully your options in the event of being compromised by civilians".

Jim knew what he meant although this kind of thing was best left to those on the ground to judge to gravity of the situation and it was better to leave it that way.

When asked, the patrol rather strangely had no questions, highly unusual, probably a reflection of the fact that the briefing had been given by the Director of Special Forces. Maybe they are just at a loss for words, contemplated Jim. Usually at Hereford there were more opinions than arseholes in the room, following any briefing.

"Well gentlemen thank you, I wish you all the very best of luck!" concluded the Brigadier.

At the end of it Jim did his best to conceal his emotions, it was good to be active after the recent delay but maybe a different approach would yield a better chance of success all round. Pointless to express any reservations though, the hard decisions had been taken. Overall Jim reasoned that the Brigadier must be under enormous pressure to assist the Task Force and was doing his job in the best way possible in the circumstances. If Jim had been in the same position what would he have done differently?

So that was it then, looking at the situation from a purely personal perspective common sense had not prevailed and here was Jim with the 7 patrol members in the back of the 4 tonner on the way to RAF Brize Norton. Somehow it still didn't seem quite real, Jim felt that he needed to pinch himself, perhaps he would wake up and it had all been a bad dream.

After weeks of waiting everything seemed to be moving on at alarming pace. On reflection it now seemed that the rush to deploy troops on the mainland was more important than correctly quantifying the actual mission. Perhaps it was all about demonstrating our political will? Maybe best leave that to the politicians, now we are in this we need to give it our best shot.

The weapons and explosives had been loaded separately and were already en-route to RAF Brize Norton. As had been outlined in the briefing the Patrol would be reunited with their equipment later in Ascension.

It was fairly quiet in the back of the 4 tonner, Jim chatted to Ed, both men seeming to avoid talking about the mission, realising at this stage there wasn't much worthwhile to say. Ed was a SSgt with 10 years SAS service. He had been one of Jim's instructors during selection. Jim liked him. He was intelligent and thoughtful and Jim respected his judgement. Ed liked to win but did so making measured calculated decisions.

Originally there had been two 4 man patrols one from Jim's troop and another troop officer leading the second, 6 and 9 Troops respectively. For various reasons, none of which was entirely clear but Jim supposed probably associated with the change from a pure reconnaissance to a hybrid reconnaissance and seek and destroy aircraft mission, 3 men from 9 Troop had been merged into Jim's patrol together with another member from his own 6 Troop.

As a result of the merger Jim had gained two vastly experienced and senior members of the team Sgt Mike and Tpr Vic. Jim guessed that in age they were somewhere between 35-38. Vic had left the regiment some years before after winning a DCM in Oman, to become RSM of his parent unit and then had made a decision to re-join the SAS. He was undoubtedly a very tough and determined man, Jim wondered whether if push came to shove would he Jim would be able to re-take and re-pass selection some 10 years on when he would be in his mid to late 30's, as Vic had done the previous year. Both Mike and Vic were excellent soldiers and of course the best men to have on ones side in a tight spot. Jim was pleased to have them on-board although he did not quite understand what drove them both. Did they really feel as gung-ho about this mission as they behaved or was it a very good act? Did they not fully appreciate the position they were in? Was it just the need for excitement, the adrenalin rush, hey everyone experienced this to some extent, but these two seemed to want it more than most. Perhaps the most difficult element to deal with was that it felt almost like they were in competition trying to outdo each other in how far they might go.

Jim felt he could be totally open with Ed even to the point of sharing some of his misgivings, for some reason he didn't feel quite the same when dealing with Mike and Vic. With Ed you knew where you stood, he was highly professional, would do everything reasonable to get the job done but at the end of the day would also like to ensure that he and the team got home. Mike and Vic unleashed would take on the whole Argentinian Army.

Also in Vic and Mike's defence they had seen action in many theatres and probably viewed Jim with the usual suspicion voiced by the old and bold about troop officers, namely, "he's just another Rupert, here for 3 years, wants to win a medal and is highly likely to drop us in the shit and get us killed in the process."

Whilst this was still the prevailing view, Jim liked to think that over the previous 2 years he had worked hard to 'fit in' showing good judgement and whenever the situation had permitted he had listed to the advice of the senior NCOs in the regiment very carefully. Not to say that this style of leadership came unnaturally to Jim he had never been the 'born to lead' type and had never expected or asked for any privileges from his officer status.

Looking round the back of the 4 tonner he watched the other 4 patrol members. They were excellent soldiers, Cpl Rob, LCpl Ian LCpl Nick and Tpr Tom. Three Paras and a former member of the TA 23 SAS respectively. All of them had more than 5 years' service in the Regiment. From some of the banter during training and planning Jim knew they had at least to some extent mixed feelings about the mission although of course none of them had openly discussed it.

The 4 tonner followed the time honoured route, to Brize Norton, Ross, Gloucester, Cirencester, again no time for a tea and bacon sandwich at the usual pit stop. They finally arrived and were met by an RAF Flight Lt at the Guard Room who escorted them into the waiting area.

"Your flight will be at 1000hrs he said cheerily, you can have some breakfast here and we will call for you at 0930hrs."

"Thanks, much appreciated" said Jim. Adding "I'm sure the boys will manage a bacon sandwich." He had a sort of 'the condemned men ate a hearty meal' feeling, he smiled certainly doing his level best not to convey this to the RAF officer.

"You'll be travelling by VC10 and we should get you to Ascension Island by tea time," he went on "there will be a fairly short stop at Dakar to refuel, you will not need to get off the plane, in fact it is far better that you all sit tight and remain on board."

"No problem" said Jim, "I guess there would be much to site-see anyway?"

"Complete shit hole" said the RAF Officer.

Despite not having much of an appetite for the past few days, along with the others Jim duly polished off a bacon sandwich and a mug of regulation strong sweet tea.

Jim recalled the advice of his old Company Sgt Major whilst in training at Sandhurst. "A good soldier will eat every meal as though it is their last." Jim managed to smile to himself when remembering the man, and despite being rather useless advice at the current time, he recounted the similar rule that had also been expounded by the same Sgt Major this time relating how to deal with girls!

At 0945hrs they climbed the steps on the VC10 all having been issued with the standard white cardboard lunchbox containing hardboiled egg, wafer thin spam sandwich made with elastic white bread and an apple. "Haute cuisine, no going back now, this is it," reflected Jim.

There was plenty of room on the plane with seemingly no other travellers, so the boys spread themselves and did their best to crash out. Before dozing off, Jim thought about the mission, in some ways maybe getting there was worst part; once they could get started their training would kick in. At the back of his mind he felt they should be preparing but to do this they needed detail that was not available, in the circumstances they would just have to call it the way they saw it, there was no other way.

Chapter 4

COBRA Whitehall London May 1982

"Thank you Brigadier, that was a most comprehensive briefing," said the Minister. The Minister was somewhat in awe of the Brigadier who was something of a legend, the most decorated soldier serving in the British Army. Not wanting to display any lack of knowledge that might cause embarrassment to himself by perhaps asking the wrong questions the Minister keenly looked round the room to judge the response of the assembled team. Seeing no response he went on.

"So where are your men now?"

The Brigadier was standing next to a map showing the Atlantic. "We have been advised that they arrived in Ascension Island about 2 hours ago, Minister. We are on track for insertion into the mainland during tomorrow night. The plan is to issue a final order for the mission to proceed after this meeting."

The Minister asked, "So how do you assess their chances of success?"

The Brigadier paused, "well as you know Minister there is a distinct lack of hard intelligence about the target and so we cannot be precise about the location or indeed the readiness and strength of the enemy forces."

The Minister was a small neat man, dressed in an expensive suit; he was meticulous and liked to involve himself in the detail. He was known in Whitehall to be highly ambitious. The Brigadier thought he was probably an improvement on the last Defence Minister; at least he displayed interest in Special Forces Operations and seemed prepared to listen. The recent course of events in the South Atlantic had thrust the Minister into the limelight. By nature he was a cautious man but catching the mood of the Nation, almost to the Brigadier's surprise, he seemed to have risen to the task. Now determined to make his mark on the conflict he had put his military options planning team under significant pressure, how could they strike at the mainland and protect the Task Force? Of course he did not want to be tainted by any failure and his experience would guard carefully against this but in the event of success he wanted it to be known he was the driving force.

"Well John, do we really have no intelligence on the target?" The Minister addressed the Director of MI6 sounding more than a little irritated.

The Director of MI6 felt uncomfortable, no one had seen this situation coming and the South Atlantic had not until very recently been on the radar. He briefly reflected on the words of Harold McMillan who when Prime Minister was asked what he feared the most and had replied "Events, dear Boy, events."

The Director knew the best he could do was to buy more time.

"Unfortunately we lack of assets on the ground and intelligence on the area is limited. Our best hope in the short term for more detailed information is that it still likely to come from the Americans who have satellite coverage of the area. As we all know given the sensitivity of the position at the UN they at least don't want to be seen to be explicitly supporting our war effort." Regaining composure he continued smoothly, "obviously we are working to remove any obstacles and hope to be given access in the near future."

The Minister looked directly at John, "You will let me know immediately if you need any help oiling the wheels further, John?"

"Of course Minister but to be honest the fewer people there are involved on both sides of the Atlantic will I think improve our chances of a significant level of cooperation with the CIA." As you know in public at least, the Americans want to be seen to be even handed."

"Very well then, I suppose we must wait for further developments." The Minister then turned his attention back to the Brigadier.

"Of course this will be too late for your men on this particular mission Brigadier, so going back to my question, how do you rate their chances?"

The Brigadier looked gravely at the assembled team. "This is probably not what you want to hear but the chances of them actually finding and destroying the aircraft must realistically be assessed as quite low. It is hard to imagine that the aircraft will not be moved from location to location on a frequent basis and heavily guarded so even if they are found, getting near enough to do damage will be hard."

All eyes were on the Brigadier. After a short pause he continued "so given this scenario we must continue to look at other options. In the best case the patrol may succeed in causing some collateral damage to the enemy. They will certainly divert energy and resources from the overall war effort. When news of the insertion leaks out or the patrol is compromised as it likely eventually will, large numbers of enemy ground troops will be used to track them down. Even if they are captured the enemy forces will continue to be paranoid about other patrols and saboteurs."

"So you are implying that even if the patrol is not successful in completing the mission from an overall campaign perspective we really don't have anything to lose," asked the Minister.

"We don't really like to see it in those terms and I would certainly not like to see it communicated in this way outside of this room, but yes I suppose that is the basic principle." The Brigadier looked round the room, and then continued.

"Of course we must understand that there is a price to be paid. We are at war and hard decisions will need to be made. We do need to balance to benefits of this mission against the risks to the men in the patrol. The aircrew, assuming we use this method of insertion will also be at considerable risk and of course we must be prepared to lose a Sea King helicopter from our fleet, hopefully you will all recall that I told you in the initial briefing that this would be a one way ticket."

The Minister looked around the room, it was getting late and he still had a mountain of paperwork to get through back in his office.

"Well gentlemen I think we have debated this enough for now. Unless there are objections I would like to sanction this mission to go ahead and also to request that the Brigadier and his staff continue planning further options."

He looked around the room; the assembled company nodded their agreement.

"Very well," Brigadier, "Please proceed with this mission. We will reconvene back here same time tomorrow. Good night gentlemen."

Chapter 5

Ascension Island May 1982

Darkness fell quickly, it was always a sudden affair in the Tropics no warning. Here they all were, lying in the open around a wooden hut at the end of the runway which had been carved out of what seemed to be a lunar landscape. Jim looked around, just about making out the outlines of the others who were crashed out on their green maggots around him. He was not sure if they were actually asleep or just like him looking up at the night sky. Jim looked up at the sky fascinated. The stars were unfamiliar, the air was still, warm and humid and there was a trickle of sweat running down his face. So this is my first time in the Southern Hemisphere, approximately 5 degrees south he thought. In different circumstances I'd really like to be able to take more of it in.

Earlier that day they had landed at Ascension in the VC10 on the airstrip which had been hastily extended to support the Task Force. Looking back at the trip it all of it seemed much of a blur. On paper it had seemed the ideal opportunity to get some rest and then perhaps to review plans with the boys. However much of the trip had passed in silence, each man seemingly in retreat with their own private thoughts.

Upon arrival the patrol had changed from their civilian clothes into uniform, or at least partly. The heat was stifling as they unpacked their personal equipment from the containers. One of the problems they faced was selecting the right kit to bring on the mission. The mission started in the UK in late spring then spanned the tropics but would end up nearer to Antarctica in early winter. In anticipation of the end game they had all taken cold weather gear. This included a gortex anorak that had been purchased locally for each man from the local Cotswold Camping in Hereford. Jim had toyed with taking it or not as it took up valuable space. In the event he decided to take it, strap it to the outside of his Bergen. It could be dumped if it became an unnecessary burden.

Jim had packed and re-packed his rations, warm kit, the sticks of C4 explosives and timer devices several times. Like the others he checked and cleaned his Armalite M16 and the backup 9mm Browning which he carried in a shoulder holster, carefully packing his spare ammunition. Nothing would seem to fit into his Bergen anymore, which he estimated at 80lb. The last minute decision for the patrol to pack explosives and timing devices meant that he and the others had needed to cut down on rations. Whatever happened, he determined the one thing he would not be leaving was his trusted green maggot sleeping bag. In difficult times even when you were soaked through this was a proven lifesaver.

A shadowy figure walked across to where his team were resting.

"Hey Boss, you awake? I've got HQ on the line they want to talk to you."

Jim moved to his feet, "OK Trev, thanks I'll be right with you."

Trev was the hastily appointed SAS Liaison officer in Ascension Island. Jim knew him fairly well, two years earlier he had been the SSM responsible for Training Wing and in particular running his SAS selection course.

"Hell Trev, I really wonder what is going to happen next on this one. Sometimes I think life has become a bit too exciting. "

"Interesting times for all of us Boss. I was talking to Ed and the boys earlier they are pretty fed up. It seems like they can't make up their mind back at HQ."

He added touching Jim on the shoulder, "just remember to take it steady on the radio now, calm down; there is no point in arguing. When you are finally deployed the level of interference should just fade away." Trev probably had some inkling as to what would be coming across the ether.

The men moved into the hut, Jim said hullo to the signals officer Tim who passed him the headset and microphone. They had worked together in Oman. Jim sat down at the desk and put the headset on and spoke into the microphone. The satellite communications were completely secure so they could speak freely without following strict voice procedure.

"Bravo 1, over"

"Hullo Bravo 1, this is control." Jim recognised the Brigadier's voice.

"Your mission is confirmed, and you will take off first light. Assuming favourable meteorological conditions we think it will take approximately 15 hours to reach the DZ in the South Atlantic. As per your previous orders you will parachute into the sea. Pick will be arranged with a Fleet Auxiliary vessel and then you will be transferred by helicopter to one of the carriers, probably to the Invincible. The Captain has already been briefed to expect you and will make the necessary arrangements for you to be flown by a Sea King tomorrow night into the mainland, again as per your orders. Roger so far over?"

"Roger," said Jim, thinking fuck this is it, up to this point there had been some kind of hope that perhaps if they were lucky they would be re-assigned to join the rest of the SAS Squadrons on operations with the Task Force.

"Any questions, over?"

"What happens to the helicopter after it has dropped us off; if it is seen or found it might increase our chances of compromise, over?"

The voice at the other end sounded a little exasperated. I suppose it was a pretty stupid question though Jim in hindsight. The slightly terse response came back "Not really your concern, we have local assets who will dispose of the evidence, over."

Pointless going on Jim thought, best not to push it any further. Thinking 'not really our concern', it's not their asses on the line. Jim decided to terminate the briefing before he said something he regretted,

"Hullo control this is Bravo 1, no further questions over."

"All that remains is for me to wish you luck and we look forward to seeing you when you get back to London, out."

Trying hard to supress any sign of emotion, Jim passed the headset and microphone back to Tim.

"Well Trev it looks like we leave here in 4 hours, best to get the wet suits ready, can you let us know when we need to get our kit loaded onto the C130? I'll go and brief the team."

At 0530hrs the patrol was ready to move, everyone had changed into their wetsuit. Given the temperature must have been about 30 degrees C, it already felt quite sticky and uncomfortable.

"Never thought I'd be wearing rubber into battle Boss," Ed said.

Ian piped up "Reckon you should ask to have the suit saved as a souvenir and then wear it in the bedroom when you get back. It'll be a real turn on especially if the happy recipient knows where it has been."

"If it's anything like mine inside it's likely to be a real turn off." Rob cut in.

"I think that's because you sweat more than the rest of us", retorted Ian.

Jim smiled even in times of uncertainty you could rely on a bit of black humour to raise the spirits. As the banter continued two land rovers came towards them in the semi-darkness.

They all shook hands with Trev who wished them well after declining the kind offer of second use of Ed's wetsuit. The patrol members loaded their bergens into the back of the open land rovers and climbed on board. The movement of the air felt cool and refreshing on Jim's face. The modified C130 was waiting at the bottom of the runway.

There was time for a brief introduction to the pilot and co-pilot. Jim shook hands with them both.

The pilot looked at Jim, "We'll be refuelling about 10 hours into the trip. This is a fairly critical time, if it goes well we should be at the planned DZ in about 13-15 hours, so you should be on the Fleet Auxiliary vessel that is scheduled to pick you up in time for tea." He joked.

"In the unlikely event we cannot refuel or we have bad weather and cannot continue my orders are to return to base and try again at the earliest opportunity."

"Fine with me," said Jim.

After a pause he continued, "In order to complete the round trip even with planned refuelling the distances are so great that we have made a few modifications inside. As you can see most of the back is filled with a giant fuel tank so the loadmaster has rigged up some stretchers for you and your team to rest on the way down. These are suspended over the fuel tank."

The pilot pointed to the suspended stretchers inside the airframe.

"Unfortunately there isn't much we can do about the fuel smell, but we will do our best to make you as comfortable as possible during the trip. Unless you have any other questions the loadmaster will supervise you getting on board and we'll need to get ready for take-off."

"No questions thanks," said Jim, looking round at the rest of the team who nodded their agreement.

"Oh one other thing, you are welcome to come up to the cockpit, no more than 2 at a time and check our position and watch the refuel. " The pilot added cheerfully before moving off.

The assisted the loadmaster and Jim and the others climbed on board. From his stretcher Jim looked across to the others suspended around him. The noise of the engines picked up and the plane started to move forward with increasing speed.

Chapter 6

South Atlantic May 1982
Jim was lying on the stretcher; it was practically on top of the large fuel tank that seemed to completely fill the back of the C130. The rest of the boys were also suspended around in various positions. It was possible to climb down and move along the side of the tank to get to the cockpit and there was a small space at the back where they had stored their kit and parachutes. Maybe the pilot had overcooked the part around the smell of aviation fuel; it really didn't seem quite so bad. Certainly nothing like the unpleasantness experienced on the practice raid on the airfield a few weeks earlier. Also as they were flying at a high altitude there was little turbulence.

Given the team were scattered and the background noise of the engines there wasn't much opportunity to chat. However there was plenty of time to reflect on the events of the past 2 days though, thought Jim. On paper this was a good time to rest too, although at least for Jim there was too much going on in his head to sleep.

It seemed hard to imagine that little over a day ago they had been in Hereford and now here they all were, some way into their journey to the South Atlantic. Less than 2 days before he'd been having a farewell pint with Snapper and Kev. Right now the future seemed a little uncertain; it was hard to imagine what it would be like parachuting into the South Atlantic. Like any other drop? Well maybe, sure they had all done plenty of parachute drops including ones into the sea. However Studland Bay in Dorset even if the water was a bit cool was a half a world away from the South Atlantic. This was also his first operational drop into a war zone. Jim wondered whether the water was really as cold and the weather as filthy as he had read. There were other doubts nagging away at him; whatever he did they just would not leave his brain. Would they be picked up and what would happen to them in the event of an air raid or bad weather? Not really having any answers to these questions, Jim decided quite logically that he should try and think about something else. At the end of the day assuming the plane reached the DZ it seemed highly likely that they would be given the green light, whatever the weather or operational situation. He thought, probably for the best anyway, we really don't want to go through this again.

Jim tried unsuccessfully to get out of his current mind set, think of rugby, home, the farm anything to switch off. Instead his brain continued to move ever forwards into the mission, assuming the drop was successful and they were transported to the carrier as planned. How easy will it be to fly 400 miles in a Sea King helicopter into the mainland, avoiding radar, possible bad weather and the missiles? Perhaps the hardest thing to accept is that for all this time you have no control over the destiny of you and your men. Thinking about this didn't help much so time to move forward he wandered onto the next stage of the mission.

OK so now suppose the helicopter insertion has been successful and here we are on the mainland. We have landed at some RV, still to be agreed with the pilot. The maps are crap and there is no accurate intelligence on the target. Finding it might be less than straightforward. What was the terrain like; were there enemy forces deployed in defence of their aircraft and would they be looking for us? Highly fucking likely, though Jim answering his own questions. The essence of this mission made planning ambushes and house assaults in Northern Ireland seem like a picnic in the park.

No, this line of thought wasn't helping much either, so time to move on. Jim imagined the patrol destroying the targets in a blaze of glory. At the moment this seemed in the realm of boys own adventure stuff but just suppose it really happened despite all adversity, then what?

Jim knew that survival was an important part of the job, at least it was for him and as far as he knew it was pretty high up on the list of priorities for the others too. He had been brought up in his Troop on some legendary stories about "Ruperts making bad decisions that good men got killed." So here they all were, the shit would have well and truly hit the fan and there was a small matter of 60 km between them and the Chilean border presumably with a significant level of interest from the natives.

Trying to cancel out the unpleasant image of being hunted from his mind he determined the only way forward was to focus on the here and now, taking literally one step at a time. Who knows something may change. This approach was more than a bit alien to him as he loved the excitement of executing a good plan even if as always things don't quite work out. He wouldn't say that he was particularly meticulous but he did at least like to be an integral part of the planning process. That way you felt ownership and it helped you to believe in the viability of what you are being asked to do. The political stakes were so great and events here were in this instance so far way out of his control and the detail so lacking for successful execution, that it was necessary to ignore training and rely on instincts to really take things one step at a time. There appeared to be no other way. The wider outcome would be pre-ordained with someone else, who was not even there, making the big decisions.

So the next big event would be the warning order to put on the parachutes as they approached the DZ.

The loadmaster can up to Jim and said "Skipper wants to know whether you want to watch the refuelling operation?"

"OK thanks," said Jim thinking what else was there to do?

Jim climbed down and made his way in the limited space between the fuselage and fuel tank towards the cockpit.

The pilot and co-pilot welcomed him cheerily into the cramped cockpit. Good guys Jim thought. Jim made an effort to smile, he realised that he could not have been smiling much recently.

"We are about 3 hours from the DZ, this next stage is critical, if we don't refuel we have to turn back," the pilot explained. It was hard to hear above the continual roar of the engines.

Jim looked ahead and saw the rear end of a huge Victor tanker. Projecting from the rear end by about 20 metres was a black hose with a funnel shaped object attached to the end.

"We need to connect to that" the C130 pilot pointed to the black funnel on the end of the hose.

Jim watched fascinated, realizing the exceptional skill that it must take to perform this manoeuvre. Both planes needing to fly in a straight slightly downward path, same speed for at least 10 minutes.

The first attempt failed, and the C130 pilot backed off for a fresh approach. The second attempt failed and Jim began to wonder whether they would make it. The options weren't too good, not if he was truthful that he felt that passionate about the mission he just didn't fancy going back to Ascension Island, getting the latest and greatest thinking on his mission all the way from London and then doing the whole thing again tomorrow.

On the third attempt they made the fuel connection, the pilot giving him the thumbs up. Jim couldn't quite find it within himself to jump up and down with joy; however he did his best to join in the celebration. Definitely mixed feelings on this one, but on the whole a good outcome he supposed. The boys must be heartily sick of the back of C130s and the smell of aviation fuel. As at least they would not be going back, on the other hand now there was definitely the parachute jump into the South Atlantic, coming soon.

He moved back down the aircraft giving the thumbs up to the team suspended above. There were a few forced smiles in the team; probably underneath they all felt the same way as him, uncertainty for sure but the best option was to go forward.

An hour or so later and the loadmaster gave Jim the nod, shouting in his ear "time to put on the parachutes and get your the containers ready. The latest news from the vessel at the DZ is that we think the weather will be suitable, there is a bit of a breeze blowing from the West but as far as we can tell nothing to worry about you should be OK."

Jim nodded and moved towards the tailgate where they had stored their T10 steerable parachutes and their equipment which had been packed into individual containers. Each container held their Bergen with essential equipment, weapons and ammunition, all carefully wrapped in an oilskin sheet. Back in Ascension Island they had done their best to ensure the contents of the bergen were waterproofed using black plastic bags. These had then been stowed into watertight containers that would be dropped separately and would be recovered from the sea at the same time as the patrol.

The others followed Jim, there seemed to be some sense of relief that they were finally about to leave the plane. It was always thus on parachute jumps, normally most people just wanted to get out of the plane, especially if there was turbulence and air sickness.

It was a little cramped but they all quickly donned the chutes, and performed the standard checks on each other. Since they were already dressed in their wetsuits it made the process quite straightforward. A bit of a milestone Jim thought. It was his first operational jump, as far as he knew probably the same for the others. On operational jumps there was normally no need for a reserve as they would jump from a low altitude to minimise time in the air. They hadn't discussed the jump height with the pilot; Jim guessed it would be as low as 450 feet, he wasn't sure, just enough time for the main chute to deploy and drop the container, certainly little or no time to deploy a reserve if there were to be any problems with the main. Mind you right now deploying reserves or otherwise wasn't really high on the list of priorities.

"We are making a run over the DZ in about 10 minutes; the Skipper has established contact with your reception vessel. So it's time to get hooked up." The loadmaster briefed the assembled team.

They stood up and fastened the hooks from their parachute onto the wire attached to the airframe of the C130. The containers were also hooked up it had been agreed that they would go out on the first run and the patrol second.

The back of the C130 opened slowly; as they peered out of the back they could see the grey South Atlantic below. The ramp was now completely down and they waited.

The containers were moved to the ramp. The lights changed from red to green and the loadmaster made the final movements as they disappeared from view. Jim could just see the open parachutes are the C130 turned for its second run.

The C130 approached the DZ for the second time.

"Red on" shouted the loadmaster.

The red light was now showing at the back of the C130.

The team moved forward to the back of the ramp. No real need for a particular order of jumping, just to get out as soon as possible and together, ensuring they were not too widely dispersed when they landed. Even if they were to go out together they would be quickly separated in the slipstream.

They were in position waiting, all staring at the green light.

"Green on" shouted the loadmaster, Jim and his patrol surged forwards off the back of the ramp. Falling yet because of the strong slip stream it almost felt like you were being carried along horizontally.

Not true of course, Jim felt the familiar buffeting, and then found himself face down towards the earth as his parachute opened in front of him. This was always a sense of relief. He slowly swung underneath the canopy giving him the opportunity to take in the surroundings.

The mass of grey sea fast approaching below and then to his relief, maybe 200-300 metres away to the left as planned a Fleet Auxilliary container ship which he assumed to be the reception vessel.

Jim looked around briefly and saw with relief that the other chutes had opened, it looked like they were all OK. No time to steer towards them. The sea was fast approaching so he placed himself, legs together elbows in and when just above the water collapsed his parachute, falling the last few feet. This helped to avoid the situation of being entangled beneath the parachute.

As he entered the water he felt the brain numbing coldness of the water. Fuck me I really don't fancy being in here to long, he though, if I ever come here again I must remember that a wet suit just doesn't really cut it. Floating to the surface he looked around for the others and for the boat. This was quite difficult as he realised that there was a huge swell, he estimated maybe the height of a house. Fortunately there was little or no wind. The experience was quite scary, when he reached the top of a wave he could see the reception vessel and some of his patrol whilst in the following depression nothing. He really hoped that the pickup crew would be on their way, it was very cold. Bad thoughts always seem to come to the fore at times like this; so what if there were to be an air raid right now? He supposed any attempt to pick them up would be put on hold, so not a happy ending then. Next thought, how deep was the Atlantic at this point? Telling himself for goodness sake shut to fuck up, this is going nowhere, just put your faith in the fact that the people tasked with picking up the patrol will do a great job.

Time passed, perhaps 10 minutes, and he was getting colder, whilst on the crest of the swell he managed to identify a lifeboat with 2 sailors rowing and a 3rd in the boat assisting in the pickups. The lifeboat had managed to pick up 3 of the team and at each viewing opportunity seemed to be getting closer. Eventually Jim felt a surge of relief as strong arms helped pull him and his equipment into the boat. Maybe not quite the welcome he had expected but nonetheless quite a relief.

Jim struggled into a sitting position.

"Fuck it's really cold Boss, which dipstick decided that we should wear wetsuits?" Then Ed continued, "I thought that being as this was being led by boat troop you would have known better."

Jim managed to smile between shivers. He was number four to be rescued, Ed, Ian and Rob were already there and there were 4 more to go. The small boat moved up and down seemingly playing now you see me, now you don't, with the grey mass of the RFA vessel Fort Austin. Slowly they moved to the remaining men, first Tom, Mike, then Vic and finally Nick.

"I'd hate to see this place on a windy day, Boss" said Ed.

"Me too Ed," said Jim. It was calm, clear and felt very cold. "I just can't get used to the size of the swell." Both were men were shivering violently.

"I'm worried about the kit it'll be a miracle if it stays dry" said Ed through chattering teeth. "Right now I could definitely use getting changed into something dry and real quick" said Jim. Looking around he saw what looked to be giant seagulls gliding above the waves.

"I've just seen my first Albatross, must remember to make a note in my diary Ed," he tried to joke.

It had taken almost 40 minutes to get Nick out of the water and he definitely looked in bad shape.

"Fuck me, any longer and I'd be on the way out." Was all Nick managed to say as he collapsed into the boat shivering.

The two sailors put their back into the rowing and the Fort Austin appeared about 100 metres away and slowly loomed ever closer. Eventually they went alongside; the swell made the lifeboat rise and fall Jim guessed about 3 metres which made the operation to hook up to the lifting gear quite difficult and dangerous. As there was a heavy metal hook swinging violently as head height. Several times it skimmed perilously close to the patrol members.

"You know this must be one of my worse experiences to date, in what can only be considered as a long and distinguished military career," joked Ed. "I'm really not sure we want to be doing this again."

"Who needs the Argies, I reckon that hook could seriously fuck up your whole day," he continued.

Eventually they swinging hooks fell under control catching the lifeboat which was slowly winched back to deck height. The patrol climbed out onto the deck, the focus of some friendly amusement from a number of the crew who had gathered to assist with their kit.

A RFA officer with several rings walked across to the party. Jim was not really familiar with how naval reserve ranks worked but the guy was clearly the most senior member of the crew around. He introduced himself as the Purser and shook hands with Jim. "Welcome to the South Atlantic, he smiled.

Between chattering teeth Jim managed "I'd like to say nice to be here but that is probably stretching the truth. Anyway thanks very much for picking us up. It was a bit worrying, we didn't know what to expect."

"I'm afraid the water is a bit too cold for a wet suit." The Purser continued, "Did anyone not brief you?" Not waiting for the answer he continued, "How are your men?"

"I think we will be OK, I'm a bit worried that the last 2 out got really cold. It will be good to get out of these wet suits as soon as possible and then check the equipment."

"OK if you all move across the deck and assemble over there. Then get yourselves changed and in about 10 minutes I'll arrange for some of my guys to help you move your kit up to the helipad. In approximately 20 minutes you are scheduled to be moved by Sea King to HMS Hermes. I don't know any other details I'm afraid, we have just been tasked to facilitate your pick up. It all seems a bit of a rush."

He paused, adding "just leave anything you don't want to take and we'll dump it."

Jim nodded. "One thing for sure, I can't wait to get out of this fucking wetsuit; I've been wearing it for about 20 hours. We started off in the tropics and now we are practically in the Antarctic, I wouldn't like to vouch for the state of the interior."

"We'll definitely be dumping that one then!" The Purser joked, he continued, "One of the lads will bring up some mugs of soup. Not sure what it's like or even in it, but I pride myself on us not wasting anything here." With that he went off.

At the mention of soup Jim realised that he probably should by now feel hungry. It was probably the best part of a day ago that he had eaten anything but he just didn't feel hungry. Not good for a soldier, he knew it was essential to eat at every opportunity. He joined the others who were busily trying to change. It looked as though despite their best efforts to waterproof everything in the containers their kit was at best damp and in most cases quite soaked.

Nothing for it but to get changed anyway, thought Jim. They had all worn wet kit for weeks in the jungle but the temperature difference didn't help much here. Maybe the wetsuit was a better option, Jim considered, quickly coming to a conclusion that no it was better to wear wet uniform.

The rest of the equipment, food, ammunition, timing devices and explosives could take the soaking. The food was packaged in more or less waterproof packaging, with the ammunition and explosives would be no worries, just get rid of the salt. I'm not so sure about the timing devices though, thought Jim, we may need to get these checked out. I'll see what Tom thinks.

Nick was doing his best to check the radio. "Not looking so good Boss, we'll need to get this baby dried out as soon as possible."

"Fuck the radio," quipped Mike, "we need to get me dried out as soon as possible before I lose my bollocks completely."

Ignoring this Jim explained, "Well lads it looks as though we are being picked up in about 20 minutes and transported by Sea King to HMS Hermes."

"Ah I remember when I was back at Hereford they say the Sea Kings have done so much flying recently that they are just falling out of the sky Boss." Ian thought he would try and cheer everyone up with some black humour, it never fails.

"Well thanks for that Ian, I'm sure we are all grateful for you letting us know this extremely useful information," said Ed.

Jim continued, "We will ask if there is anywhere we can dry out essential items of kit including the radio as a priority, when we get to Hermes. In the meantime we need to pack up best we can and head for the helipad." Jim pointed to the upper deck.

Moving the kit up 2 flights of narrow metal ladders to the helipad was quite difficult, but it did have the advantage of helping them all to keep warm. It seemed like not one of them could have assembled a dry uniform between them. It would take quite a while to get dry using body heat unless they could find some special facilities. This might not be so easy down here, such luxury would be hard to come by and everyone seemed preoccupied with their daily business rather than worry over such trifling problems as wet kit.

They waited on the helipad for the Sea King to appear. It was just starting to get dark the sky had become overcast and there was now a cold wind blowing.

The Sea King appeared skimming low over the waves. It hovered over the helipad and touched down. They waited for the loadmaster to give the signal and approached in the normal way from 2 o'clock direction.

Once aboard they quickly took off and Jim presumed were on their way to the Hermes. Looking out of the back he could see the waves below and the ever present Albatrosses skimming the waves. Thinking privately, that on first impressions this was a godforsaken place. Jim reflected that each new experience on the mission had so far been more unpleasant than the previous one. So it was with some trepidation that he wondered how the next stage of the mission would pan out and what surprises were in store, especially when they had re-established communications with Hereford who would no doubt get their direction from London. If the last few weeks had been anything to go by, they needed to standby for more changes!

Chapter 7

HMS Hermes May 1982

Through the rear door of the Sea King Jim could see the huge grey mass of the Hermes. He had never been on or even so close to an aircraft carrier before. Another first for the diary entry he thought.

The helicopter landed and they all dismounted. The deck was completely clear of aircraft although there was a bustle of activity.

A naval Lieutenant came forward and introduced himself to the team. Despite being on operational duty he looked smart in his uniform. No relaxation of standards here thought Jim who was damp and dishevelled and had purposely left any badges of rank back in Hereford.

The Lieutenant having eventually determined that Jim was the Troop commander, shook hands, "The Captain would like you see you immediately, one of my men will look after your team. We have cleared a bit of a space for you below."

"Fine," said Jim, "just one request perhaps in the meantime we can receive some assistance to help us dry out our kit, this would be a great help. We would also appreciate any help in checking out our radio which got wet in the drop," added Jim.

"The Chief will do what he can to help," nodding to the man standing beside him. "So if that is everything perhaps you could come with me please."

Jim left his Bergen and M16 rifle with the patrol keeping for some reason his 9mm pistol tucked inside his SAS smock, adding "see what you can do Ed to help get the contents dried out."

He followed the naval officer who was about his age; he seemed quite a nice guy. Jim had never been on a warship before let alone on one on operational duty and so immediately found the experience of moving around a real eye opener. There was a seemingly endless series of steel bulkhead doors probably every 4 metres or so. On moving through the ship one would climb through the door ensuring it was always sealed behind. Being tall was a real drawback. The doors appeared always to be manned by a sailor whose task it was to ensure the door stayed shut in the event of an emergency. So you really would not want to be on the wrong side of the door in the event of a drama, there would be absolutely nothing you or anyone else could do, reflected Jim. He always had a slight discomfort for events that were not at least in some way within his control or those of his team or so he felt an instant respect for the men with gloves and flash masks whose duty it was to man these doors, never seeing light of day, not even knowing what was going on above.

As they hurried along the narrow corridors ducking through bulkhead doors, Jim's companion said "I don't really know what you guys have planned but it seems to be hellish important, especially as the Captain has asked for you. Normally this sort of stuff gets delegated well down the line."

Eyeing Jim up and down he added, "From what I understand you have all arrived in a pretty unconventional way too!"

"Well I must admit that I'd prefer not to do that again, at least not in a wet suit, the water is really cold. To be honest we were not really prepared for just how cold," said Jim.

He continued, "So what's he like, the Captain I mean?" Jim figured the question was probably largely immaterial as he would find out soon enough but any information would be useful and it was a good way of engaging with his guide.

"Well I like him, he's got a sharp mind, pretty hot on detail, very strict on discipline but everyone thinks he is fair. If you can present a clear logical argument he will listen but you only have a few sentences are you never going to get more than one go at it."

"Sounds pretty much like a mirror image of our CO back in Hereford, actually not back in Hereford any more, I thought he might be here on board?" said Jim. He was thinking it would be helpful to understand his own CO's perspective on their mission, all the real crap seemed to have started at Hereford when the Boss had gone off with D and G Squadrons to join the Task Force. The hard edged judgement and incisive decision making was definitely missing.

"I'm not too sure, but think I think most of your colleagues are on Invincible at the moment," replied his guide.

"OK well no problem, all busy of course," Jim had presumed that at some stage he would likely meet up with the D and G Squadron boys or perhaps even the CO.

They climbed some stairs and finally reached the bridge and entered. First impression was that it reminded Jim of the bridge on Star Ship Enterprise; there were steel cabinets, display screens and panels of lights all manned by operators. Sitting slightly back from the main display in a large swivel chair sat the Captain.

He swung round, definitely seeming a bit like Captain Kirk at least in his current pose and looked at Jim whilst remaining seated.

"Good evening sir," said Jim.

"Good evening, you chaps certainly seem to have appeared out of the blue. According to my most recent communication you are Captain Jim XXXX, in command of a team of 7 special forces soldiers."

"That is correct sir," replied Jim.

"It seems like what you are being asked to do is such high priority that I am going to lose a Sea King helicopter and its crew."

Before Jim could reply, he continued, "We are aware of the importance and will naturally be doing do all we can to assist in your mission. Now tell me what kind of condition are you all in after the parachute drop?" The captain looked directly into Jim's eyes.

"The team are OK sir; the last ones out of the water were pretty cold as the pickup operation understandably took quite a while. More seriously our main problem is wet equipment, specifically our Satellite radio set. We will need to get this dried and checked out and working as soon as possible. I think most of the other damage is fairly superficial, probably nothing that can't be fixed in a few hours in a dry environment."

The captain nodded, "We might not have that much time. It seems that you might not know this yet Jim, but our instructions from London are to transfer you and your team to the Invincible immediately, from there you will be flown into the Mainland, tonight," he emphasised tonight. I understand that you have already been briefed on this part." He then continued, "This is going to be a one way trip for you and the aircrew we have selected. Well, at least there will be no way back to the Task Force. We really can't afford to lose men and helicopters on a whim so we do need to get it right."

Jim tried not to display any emotion; there had been no mention of actual timings in his briefings. After the past 24 hours he had expected maybe a short pause, perhaps some improved intelligence even a little recovery time, before the mission. It would be even better to catch up with his SAS colleagues get their perspective and become acclimatised. Of course that was all only nice to have but bottom line it still did not make sense to start out on the mission with no radio and potentially duff kit. He also wanted to work out a detailed plan of action with the aircrew; just maybe they would have access to better maps.

Jim felt physically drained and he was sure the others felt the same way however trying not to show it he pulled himself together, looking at the Captain said,

"Yes sir, of course we will physically be able to deploy tonight." He continued, "My main concern is that we should at least get the essential items of equipment including out satellite communications dried out and working to be operationally effective. You might be aware that unfortunately we have very little intelligence relating to the target and so going in unprepared would seem to me to further minimise our chances of success."

The Captain nodded in agreement, "Thank you for you assessment, I'm going to inform London that your mission is delayed by 24 hours. We will therefore plan on the insertion tomorrow night. As you say we need to ensure your equipment is fully dried out and I'm also thinking that your men could use some rest after your recent adventures."

He went on, "Assuming there are no further changes, you will be spending the night on board and should be prepared to move across to the Invincible first light tomorrow."

The Captain continued, "You should get back to your men and sort out your equipment. See what you can do to get dried out and then get some food and rest. I wish you and your team well for the rest of your mission."

Then addressing the Lieutenant, who had been quiet throughout the meeting, he said "Make sure that Jim and his men are looked after."

"Of course sir," replied the Lieutenant.

"Thank you sir," said Jim.

Jim and his escort made their way back through the steel bulkhead doors, which as before were always carefully sealed shut behind them. The descended two levels, and eventually after moving through a labyrinth of corridors re-joined the rest of the patrol. Here they had been given an area in what seemed like a corridor where they could set out their kit and get organised for the next stage of the mission. I hope they don't ask me to find my way back without an escort, thought Jim.

"Hey Boss," said Ed, "what do you think of our basha? At least it's dry, definitely an improvement."

The boys had stretched out some of their kit across the top of the Bergens in an attempt to get it dry.

"Nick is working with the Chief to get the radio dried out and checked."

"What's the latest Boss," asked Vic.

Jim called the team together, "we can brief up Nick when he gets back." Looking around the team, he said,

"Slight change of plan, believe it or not originally we were schedule to fly into the mainland tonight, I only discovered this whilst talking to the Captain. I've explained that we need some time to sort out communications and dry out our equipment. The Captain agreed and has therefore decided to postpone the insertion into the mainland by 24 hours. He will be advising London accordingly."

"The plan remains the same in that we will still take a one way Sea King flight into the mainland tomorrow night. We will get moved across to Invincible first light tomorrow. This gives us the opportunity to meet up with the aircrew and review our plans with them. I'm hoping they have some more up to date maps."

Jim paused, looking round at the team. Spirits had lifted a little; it seemed that everyone was pleased that they had a bit more time to prepare. Straight into Patagonia hopefully dodging the radar and ground to air missiles, after climbing out of the South Atlantic only hours previously did seem to be pushing it a bit even for this team.

"Do you really think the aircrew will have better maps than us Boss," asked Vic.

"We still have no fucking idea what the target or the area round it looks like," he continued.

"All I can say is that I bloody well hope so Vic," said Jim.

"In the meantime let's work on getting everything straight, ready for first light tomorrow, by the way I can't remember the last time I ate anything, how do we get fang, has anyone explained?"

As was his habit Jim ate with the team, he thought that in his current state, creased and still damp he was not likely to pass off as a Rupert anyway. Not that he cared anyway. He reflected on previous contact with the Navy when once during a period of diving training at Horsea Island the troop had all stayed in HMS Nelson. Not having enough time between breakfast starting and transport leaving, to change, Jim had wandered into the Ward room to grab an early breakfast wearing a tracksuit. He had been the only one there and all seemed to be well when after 10 minutes and eating his eggs and bacon an immaculately dressed Lieutenant Commander had walked over to Jim, introduced himself and then spouted forth on required standards of dress, even at breakfast.

The mess area was crowded, noisy and hot. Food was quite acceptable; in fact definitely he had eaten worst whilst on selection back in Hereford. This time he felt hungry and managed to eat a reasonable meal, pie, chips and peas. To get somewhere to sit they had to split up. The Naval ratings seemed cheerful enough and a one or two made an effort to speak to Jim and Ed. They seemed to be used to Army personnel passing through so when Jim said the team were en route to join up with the rest of the Special Forces team on Invincible, the purpose of their visit was not questioned further.

Back in their temporary base they had a visit from the Naval Lieutenant. "We need you to be ready to move at 0530hrs local tomorrow so I'll be here to give you a shout at 0500hrs. I think we explained what to do in the event of Action Stations; you just go to the assembly point down the way. Is there anything else you need?"

"No thanks, you have been very helpful. Please thank the Chief for his help too. It looks like our radio has checked out ok although we can't test it properly until tomorrow."

The boys were arranging their damp green maggots and Jim would also have confessed to feeling weary. Looking back, the past 24 hours had been eventful and yet here they were still in one piece. The future seemed uncertain, but let's all take it one day at a time. There was still a slight air of unreality about the whole business; each day that passed seemed to bring them a little nearer serious shit, always getting worst not better. Jim wondered how long this trend might go on for, perhaps if he pinched himself he would really wake up back in Hereford. No chance, need to take this hour by hour, events are so way far out of your control it's just not worth worrying about.

Jim unrolled his maggot, slightly damp, not too bad really. He's slept in worst. Great items of kit, rather heavy and bulky but they would keep you warm even if they were wet. Most of the boys were already asleep or at least were making an effort. Jim lay awake wondering what lay ahead. He had joined the regiment for some adventure and now he had it in spades; the thing he liked least was the total lack of control, with his men and him being moved around like pawns. He reminded himself that he certainly wasn't the first soldier nor would he be the last to think this. So just how the fuck did I end up here? He drifted into a disturbed sleep determined to focus on happier times.

Chapter 8

Leave 1980

A few months after the completion of his SAS selection course and first deployment with the Squadron, Jim returned home on a short period of leave. He met one of his old school mates Jack in the local pub. It was always a bit of a competition with Jack whether it was sport, academics, chasing girls or just drinking so they downed several beers in record time catching up, in particular discussing girls and the state of English Rugby, before eventually the conversation moved on the Army.

Jim was happy, although it was March and cold outside he was sun tanned from his recent visit to Oman. He was lean and very fit and having recently joined the Squadron was now beginning to feel like he belonged there. Life was good.

Maybe it was the suntan or the beer or a bit of both, anyway his mate Jack asked "So what was it like doing SAS selection?"

Usually when one of them encountered a problem they would always bluff and under play it, pretending it had all been simple. "I'd like to say it was a piece of piss but truthfully, I found parts of it very hard," said Jim.

He continued, "Firstly you never really know what to expect, there appears to be no set agenda so you get asked to do something, never knowing what may follow. This seems to freak some soldiers who are used to standard military discipline ruling their lives, being directed from one minute to the next. No one shouts or makes you do anything; in fact it is made very easy for anyone who doesn't want to play anymore to go back to their parent unit. Emphasis on self-discipline is the key, maybe a bit different from everyone's image of the army. " Jim paused for more lager before continuing.

"Then I suppose there is the physical bit, it is very demanding. If you are unlucky you can easily get injured, what the Training Officer so eloquently calls "your body letting you down." Also it is kind of related to what we have just discussed, because of the uncertainty, you really do need to always have something in reserve, although you'll never know how much. The selection course goes on for six weeks and really you never get the chance to recover. Day after day, you are just told to parade at a certain time with all your maps, the minimum kit and a Bergen that must meet the specified weight when you finish the day's exercise. During the course your Bergen weight starts off at 35lbs and goes up in increments to 56lbs. You always carry a rifle weighing 8 lbs."

Jack listened carefully, sipping his beer.

Jim continued, "Normally parade times are at some god awful hour so as to get a nice early start somewhere in the Brecon Beacons, Black Mountains or if you are really lucky the Elan Valley. You don't know which location in advance. After a long ride in the back of a 4 tonner you get dropped off and just get fed a map reference to the next RV, when you arrive there you get another, one RV after another, they just tell you to make you best time. Everything must be completed as an individual no teamwork. You never really know whether you are going fast enough but if you do go all out you run the risk of burning out and not finishing. After a few days the physical routine seems to get to a lot of people and they decide they have had enough. One day they just don't get up and parade and they are gone when you get back. As you can imagine it is quite physical and you get lots of blisters and aches and pains but I think the experience really transcends the physical effort, you see plenty of men built like brick shit houses that don't make it. I think it is more a state of mind, no matter what the bastards ask you to do you must be up for it. The whole thing culminates in a series of timed marches run continuously over a 6 day period. The last one is a real beast, endurance march, 40 miles over the Beacons with 56lb pack and rifle. Depends on the weather but you really need to finish in better than 20 hours."

"So how many people take the course and where do they come from?" Jack asked.

Buy me another pint and I'll tell you," Jim drained his glass grinning at Jack who got the message he was lagging and so also finished his pint before wandering off to the bar.

Jack duly returned with 2 pints of lager. "Pete the barman reckons he would have ordered another barrel if he had known you were coming back, can you give him a bit of notice next time?" Jack grinned and then continued.

"So come on tell me where do these people come from how many people pass?"

Jim took slug of his fresh pint, "There are 2 courses run each year, generally made up of volunteers from the Army although it is possible to get a small number from the other services. On my course we started out with about 236 soldiers of which 30 were officers. After the initial selection that's what I've just described we went down to 30 including 6 officers. But then after officer's week we went down to 3 officers."

"So what's officer's week," asked Jack.

"Basically before proceeding on the SAS training officers have a separate assessment. There are a number of exercises involving reconnaissance, combat appreciations, planning and giving orders. You present to an assembled audience from the Brigadier and CO downwards, generally it is considered quite a sporting occasion for some of the old and bold to ask young potential officers some searching questions. This can be quite daunting for most of us, given the seniority and level of experience in the room.

"How many people are in the room?" Jack seemed interested.

"About 30 or so it varies a bit, depends who is around. It goes on for about 5 days, most of it spent running around the Hereford countryside day and night, getting back in time to prepare and deliver your orders or making a presentation. You don't end up getting much sleep."

He then added, "I suppose as well as testing your resourcefulness and competence it is a fairly good way to see if your face will fit within the regiment."

"Is that it then, so after all this you have passed? Asked Jack.

"No that's just the first stage," said Jim. "It kind of gets a bit harder at least in parts. The next stage is what they call continuation training."

Pausing he drained his glass, prodded Jack to do the same. "My shout," he said wandering off to the bar.

When he returned with the refills he got the obvious question, "So what happens in continuation training?"

"Sure you want to know?"

"Yes," Jack said, "The whole thing sounds quite crazy, I always knew you had a screw loose, why would you want to do this to yourself?"

Jim continued, not really answering the second question directly.

"It last about 4 months and is split into four stages. First one covers some basic field craft, things like SAS tactics, helicopter drills, first aid, range work, signals and demolitions. It's kind of a refresher course with some SAS extras thrown in."

Jim paused, "By the way shall we move on after finishing these?"

"OK by me, let's go into town," said Jack. "But first I want you to finish off telling me about getting into the SAS."

"Why, are you interested in signing up then?"

"No don't be daft, I just curious that's all."

Jim said, "OK I'll speed things up a bit, don't want our beer to get warm do we?"

"Right where did I get to, ah yes next is jungle training. Well we went to Belize. Most of the jungle is what they call secondary, really thick vegetation. I think of everything we ever did at the end of the day this probably won out in the unpleasantness stakes."

"How do you mean" asked Jack.

"Well for starters at risk of stating the fucking obvious it is really hot and sticky, you are carrying about 70lbs minimum when out of the base camp so sweat pretty much all the time. You feel like shit and it is very easy to get dehydrated or worst still some unpleasant disease. For example they reckon that one in every 20,000 sand fly bites can infect you with leishmaniasis, it can develop into a nasty ulcer that won't heal and then starts rotting away your flesh. One of the troop commanders got it a while back and it practically finished him, nasty side effects to the treatment."

"What you said about dehydration I thought it pissed with rain most afternoons in the rain forest," said Jack.

"Smug git you always did think you were good at geography," said Jim.

Who then went on, "Well it does, maybe not every day but quite often with lots of big fat rain. The problem is the limestone base to the forest means there is very little surface water. Everyone in a patrol starts off by carrying a gallon of water each but when you sweat your cobs off just moving a few kilometres it doesn't take very long to drink it." A short pause for more refreshment and he continued.

"At least we are not going to die of dehydration, alcohol poisoning perhaps" he laughed before continuing.

"Once we were so desperate that we found a small pool of water in a fissure in rock. It was full of crap, leaves and there were terrapins in the bottom. So I was thinking the whole fucking thing must be ripe with terrapins shit and piss, come to think of it probably one and the same for a terrapin. Anyway we were desperate so just added twice the normal allocation of water purification tablets and drank the stuff. Seem to recall it made quite good tea."

"Seems to me like you are still drinking beer to help forget the taste," said Jack.

"There are a quite a few other problems," Jim continued. "You generally don't feel on top form, all your energy seems to get sapped away, so moving through some heavy undergrowth is a real effort. The terrain is difficult, it's not flat and there are some heavy duty razor backed ridges. The maps are not the best, mostly generated from aerial photographs so you need to rely on dead reckoning, time, distance and compass bearings, to work out your locations. You can't see any further than the next tree, you can't just wander off for a dump, and it's so thick you would never find the others again. Shouting is not an option as you would give away your position to any enemy. If you go uphill you can suddenly find yourself at the top of a ridge with a massive cliff in front of you."

"So what sort of stuff did you do there?" asked Jack.

"Mostly patrolling and jungle tactics, lots of live firing; we practiced our ambush drills close to the Guatemalan Border."

"How long were you there for?" Jack couldn't seem to stop asking questions.

"Not sure I should be telling you all this, might have to kill you," joked Jim.

"About 6 weeks said Jim continuing, "and if you ask me if I washed during the time in the jungle the answer is no. Basically the principle being that if you use any detergents, soap or for example toothpaste the enemy will be able to smell you and from quite a distance.

Jack looked disgusted, "So are you telling me that you didn't brush your teeth, that's so disgusting. No wonder you have such a low level of success with the ladies."

"It's true, the smell bit but not the ladies" Jim quickly qualified. "Once it pissed down solid for 2 days, my patrol was so wet that we were all actually cold and shivering, you wouldn't think it possible. I put on a dry jumper at night; I was carrying it as a reserve just in case. It had been in a plastic bag in the bottom of my Bergen. Probably it had been last washed in Persil. When I got it out the smell was really overpowering, even to me so you can imagine that someone who spends a lifetime operating in the jungle would be able to smell you a mile off. Wearing that in an ambush would be a real no, and potentially could create some drama. Anyway when we eventually got lifted out the RAF guys picking us up must have wondered what the hell they had done to deserve getting the job."

"Do you think they needed respirators," asked Jack.

"Great guys," said Jim, "Couldn't fault them, brilliant sense of humour. They insisted on inviting one of the other officers and me for a beer, sat down with us in our rancid kit, all before we had a shower!"

"Must be hard enough just to survive day to day without having to worry about the enemy" Jack added. "So what happened at the end?"

"Well our numbers reduced still further, we wound up with 13 solders left, including 2 officers."

"So what next then," asked Jack.

"Sure you want to do this now we could move on?

Jack nodded.

If we stay I reckon we definitely need to get another beer first." Jim drained his glass and handed it to Jack, who did the same and obligingly went off to the bar.

The beers arrived, Jim took a quick sip.

"Right so here we are now, back in Hereford, end of October, all skinny, lean and mean, I think I lost over a stone. It's quite cold but we move straight into something called combat survival training, this lasts for a month. Firstly you get taught some Robinson Crusoe type survival skills which are pretty useful, plants and fungi you can eat, fishing and trapping techniques. Starts off with a few lectures and visits but very soon things start to get a bit more painful. The idea being that the survival skills will help you if you were trying to evade capture if you were behind enemy lines. They also teach you some resistance to interrogation drills and things to do and not to do if you get captured."

"What kinds of things do they cover on resistance to interrogation" asked Jack.

"Well I suppose most of it is fairly common sense, try not to be antagonistic or you will surely get an even worst kicking. If you say nothing you'll also be likely get so badly beaten that you probably won't survive. The old teaching used to be name, rank and number only, but that's really the start point. Remember you need to focus on surviving and if possible to escape, so there is a balance, if you say nothing you'll likely get the shit knocked out of you. A slow release of a few details will mean that anything the enemy do get will be of limited use and you may just survive. Can't say I fancy it, best to never get caught," he grinned at Jack and then continued.

"Anyway the whole thing culminates with being hunted for 5 days, with nothing to eat in the middle of Wales in November. Essentially you get very cold and wet, and try hard not to get caught. The Robinson Crusoe stuff isn't really that useful as there isn't too much to eat. Everyone gets caught in the end and then you get carted off to an interrogation centre for 2 days. You get a minor roughing up, nothing too serious. The professional interrogators from the Intelligence Corps are set loose on you for a number of interviews, definitely slimy bastards. Problem is you are pretty weak and hungry so that eventually the boundaries between exercise and reality start to blur, you begin by thinking that I'm only here for 2 days so what, do your worst. It's very unpleasant; you are always really cold, shivering all the time in some ill-fitting suit like pyjamas, with blindfolds, stress positions and white noise. After a while you do start to think you might be going mad. During the interrogations a seed gets planted that the bastards really will keep you indefinitely.

"Anything that particularly sticks in your mind?" asked Jack.

"Well apart from the nagging doubt that they will keep you there indefinitely, you mean?"

Jack nodded.

"Well I had my hands tied behind my back and some bastard started poking around with a pencil, then shoved it up my arse before using it to look in my mouth. Even now I'd love to catch up with him. Not nice," he grinned at Jack. "At the end of it you think thank fuck that's over."

"Overall a more unpleasant experience than the jungle then?" asked Jack.

"Probably not, no at the time I likened being in Belize to Devil's Island" said Jim. Visions of carrying logs through thick mud came back in a flash.

"So moving swiftly on, the next parts of the process are actually fairly straightforward, providing you don't mind parachuting," continued Jim.

"By the way by this stage we are now down to 6 of us left in total, from the original 236, only one officer left, that's me." He said proudly.

"Sounds like they have piss poor judgement!"

"Piss off, you can always try, anyway as I mentioned what comes next is no great shakes, you go on a final exercise somewhere in Wales and this is followed by the static line parachute course at RAF Brize Norton. All pretty steady really, living in nice conditions, no pencils and a few beers most nights. If you are really lucky there are a few ladies in the mess to talk to. You do the regulation 8 jumps and its back to the regiment to join your Squadron. First jump is the worst as it is from a balloon and you just drop for 180 feet before your shute opens"

"You are actually a member of the regiment when you finish this then?" asked Jack.

"Yes sort of on probation, but this is the really scary part, actually joining the Squadron. The standard advice is to remember that things were probably working perfectly well before you arrived on the scene. So I went for the low impact approach, listened to the experience around me rather than behaving like a twat, mind you I suppose it is a bit of a fine dividing line. They could easily think so what use is this guy too.

"Must have been difficult for you then?" said Jack.

Jim ignored him and continued, "On the plus side you do actually get to wear the beret and SAS wings. My mate Phil reckoned as soon as he passed he was going to get his portrait painted and then he would jack it all in; said it would be too dangerous to hand around. He's still there of course!"

"Well having listened to this lot I still think you must be slightly mad, and that's after a fair amount of beer" said Jack.

"I prefer to get my kicks out of playing rugby every week. What's in it for you?"

Jim thought for a bit, he hadn't really considered this before.

"Well I suppose it is the opportunity to work with some great guys; some of whom are legendary. Like everything else you get good times and bad but there is the general feeling of excitement, always on edge waiting for something to happen, a permanent high, better than any drugs. Most of all it feels so good, being able to belong and be accepted by the rest of the team. Be an accepted member of the exclusive club. When you are back you can mix and drink with the circles that talk softly and laugh loudly in the pubs and clubs. You know how it feels to be an integral part of a good rugby team well this is like that only better, sounds stupid but kind of like reaching the ultimate in acceptance."

"Not so sure about that, I imagine there could be a high price to be paid for this, the worst that will happen to me is that I get a bit roughed up on a Saturday, you probably never know what they will ask you to do or where it will all end up." Jack added.

"Definitely a risk worth taking, no question," said Jim.

With that they downed the last of their pints and bid farewell to Pete the barman and headed off to town in search of further refreshments and maybe some fresh adventures.

Chapter 9

HMS Invincible May 1982

Jim was awakened by someone shaking his arm. The naval officer escort had been as good as his word. It was 0500hrs and they were scheduled to fly onto Invincible at 0530hrs. Surprisingly he had managed to sleep for a few hours and actually felt dry. Jim woke Ed who alerted the rest of the team.

"What's the weather like then, Chris?" asked Jim. He had only recently discovered his escorts name yesterday.

Not too bad, cold and quite clear, surprisingly little wind, at least for down here, a good day for helicopters" Chris replied. "I've arranged for some tea before you go. If we are quick we should make it and still have time to get you on deck."

"Sounds good to us, just need a quick piss first" said Ed.

"OK we can go via the heads" and with that they wandered off with Chris.

20 minutes later they were on deck at the ready, watching the Sea King from Invincible approaching low over the water. Jim and his team shook hands with Chris, who wished them luck on the next phase of their mission.

"Thanks," said Jim, adding "I reckon we may need it."

As the Sea King touched down they waited for the thumbs up from the pilot, following the standard drill running towards the main door at 2 o'clock to the helicopter.

Once aboard, the helicopter took off immediately and was flying just above the level of the waves for what seemed about 5 minutes when it began the approach to the Invincible. There was a hive of activity on-board but as they dismounted they were again met by yet another Lieutenant.

"Welcome to Invincible, I'm Simon, your escort."

Same drill I expect thought Jim. Here we go I bet we go and meet the Captain. These people are very well organised.

Jim introduced himself and shook hands.

"I'll arrange for your men to be taken below for some breakfast. You can join them after we go and see the Captain."

"He just wants to eyeball you and check out everything is in good shape ready for tonight. I've only heard a few whispers of what you boys are attempting and I must say we are tremendously impressed. Don't envy you one bit." Simon continued, "If you could follow me, I get you back to your men later."

The same drills were observed whilst moving through the Invincible as had been followed on Hermes. The same ritual of opening and closing the bulkhead doors as they moved down seemingly endless corridors. When they arrived at the bridge it seemed déjà vu, Starship Enterprise again only bigger and better.

The Captain swivelled around in his chair.

"Good morning sir," said Jim.

"Well I can't say I'm happy to be losing a helicopter and aircrew, but I know what you have been asked to do" said the Captain. "So tell me what kind of shape are you all in, I heard that you needed some time to dry out."

"Much better now, sir, thank you" said Jim. "I would say we are fully operational."

"Excellent, you have a busy day ahead. I want you to meet up and to work closely with the aircrew that have been assigned to your mission. No doubt there are some significant details to tie up."

"Yes sir," said Jim.

"Well we have assigned Jeff and his team, navigator and loadmaster; they actually volunteered for the task. Excellent crew, if anyone can get you in, they can."

"I'm pretty sure I know Jeff, sir," said Jim. "We were on the same JDSC course, only last year."

"Excellent, now we are going to strip down the helicopter to absolute bare essentials. Given the extreme range we need to get as much fuel on board as possible. Taking off might be bit sticky so to give you maximum lift we will be moving at maximum speed 32 knots into the wind. Once you are in the air you should be fine."

"OK sir, thanks," said Jim wondering whether he really wanted to know the fine detail or the risks involved. He had always kind of assumed a take-off was a take-off, something he had done 100s of times before.

The Captain continued, "In order to give you the best opportunity on the mainland we have asked Jeff to try and ditch the helicopter in the sea. If the wretched thing turns up in Chile the next thing you know you'll have all the Argentinian ground Forces on red alert which will make your life difficult."

"That's very reassuring sir," said Jim, afterwards hoping he didn't sound facetious.

"What kind of information do you have about your target?" asked the Captain.

"Unfortunately it is very limited sir," said Jim

"How do you mean?" asked the Captain.

"The only planning materials we have so far are old maps very large scale, no real detail, and a couple of aerial photographs I believe we obtained from the Americans. We were hoping that the aircrew might have something better," said Jim.

"I'm not so sure about that," replied the Captain, "I suspect they were hoping that you would have better maps."

He continued, "Not too much more we can do at this stage, I think you need to get off now and meet Jeff and his team. I'd like to wish you and your team the best of luck for your mission,"

"Thank you, sir," replied Jim, privately thinking we'll likely fucking well need it.

Jim was led away by Simon, to join his team. They were in the small operations room used by the aircrew and the Special Forces teams.

Jim saw Giles the OC G Squadron 22SAS, who greeted him cheerily. Giles obviously had a lot on his plate as many of his Troops were already deployed in reconnaissance missions in the Falklands. Giles didn't seem too aware of the details of the B Squadron mission so Jim was running through the details when he was aware of someone standing next to him,

He recognised Jeff immediately, it was the first time they had met since JDSC. The two men shook hands.

Jeff explained that he was going to be the pilot for the mission.

"Good to see you again, Jeff, how come you have landed up with this little job." Jim asked.

"I knew you were coming," he joked. "I really used to enjoy those evening session in the bar at Warminster."

"So did I," said Jim, thinking about slightly happier times.

"Seriously we volunteered," Dick went on. "The Squadron leader asked for volunteers so I discussed it with Will and Roy who had also volunteered and they agreed we should give it a go."

"Nice one, we couldn't be in better hands. Hell of way to get back to England though Jeff" said Jim.

Jeff introduced Will the navigator and Roy loadmaster to Jim and his team. They also met Jeff's Boss who greeted Jim with "so you are the chaps who are losing me a helicopter and one of my best aircrews." He smiled at Jim who shook hands and smiled back doing his best to be cheerful. What with the uncertainty and knowing they would all be flying out in about 8 hours he would not want to admit it but the whole business was a bit stressful.

"Beats goal keeping anytime" said Jeff.

"What's goal keeping?" asked Jim.

"Well it's kind of damage limitation, in the event of an action stations if there is a risk of Exocet attack the aircrew take it in turns to fly the helicopter round the carrier to attract the missile away from the main target. Great option, I suppose you wouldn't know too much about it," he added with a smile.

"I see said Jim" not fancying it much, "think I'll stick to what I know best."

They grabbed a tea and moved into a cramped briefing area.

"Well what information have you got?" asked Jeff.

Jim showed Jeff the maps and photographs they had.

"Not so great then" Jeff replied, adding that from his perspective the maps they had were good enough for him to be confident they would be able to get the patrol to a drop off near Rio Grande.

"We were kind of hoping that you would be able to help us with better quality maps" said Jim. "From our perspective the lack of detail on the ground combined with limited intelligence on enemy forces makes planning a bit difficult."

Jeff, Jim and the patrol members crowded round the map.

After about 30 minutes of analysis of the aerial photographs Jeff is confident with a little luck he can get them into a position off what looks like a farm track about 10km from the target, Rio Grande. Understanding precisely where the proposed drop off is located on the map is difficult, just a blob on a black and white paper. There is some concern over what looks like possible nearby habitation; perhaps some buildings but no-one can be certain.

The patrol and aircrew agreed that in the circumstances this was the best drop off point. It was not too far from the target and appeared to be findable, at least to Jeff and Will.

Jeff explained his plan for inserting the patrol.

"The take-off will be one of the most dangerous aspects given the weight. Invincible will move to a position from where the Helicopter will be able to reach the mainland with a little fuel left over. "

He pointed to area slightly NW of the West Falkland Island.

"The helicopter will be stripped down and all unnecessary weight removed. Insulation and seating will be removed from the back. This is to accommodate the additional weight of fuel. You'll be provided with survival suits and will need to sit on the floor with your equipment." Jeff continued.

"Invincible will go at maximum speed into the wind to help increase lift at take-off. When we take off we will fly due west, low level over the sea, say between 50-200ft in an attempt to avoid detection by enemy radar, ships and ground stations."

"When we get near land, Jim you can wear a headset so that we are all in communications. When we hit the coastline Will's task is to attempt to find a reference point so that we can reset our navigation aid."

"I don't know anything about the state of the air defences but based on our knowledge of equipment procurements we need to assume they have a fairly strong ground to air missile capability so we need to stay low, doing our best to avoid radar detection. Over land we will be using Passive Night Goggles (PNG) and will need to fly slowly to avoid obstacles. There is insufficient fuel to make repeated attempts so we can only make one attempt at the drop off."

"We need to determine our action on compromise at the primary drop off (DOP)," said Jim.

Earlier the patrol had discussed what actions to take, "In the event of a compromise at the primary DOP we reckon we need to put some distance between ourselves and the enemy. We want you to drop us off somewhere near the border. If things get hot we can lie low, all being well we can move on foot to the target when the heat has died down." He continued, "Obviously this adds some risk given the distances involved but on balance it may be our only option." The decision had been taken in best SAS troop traditions by a democratic vote, 6 to 2 in favour of a secondary DOP near the border. As Jim anticipated Vic and Mike were pretty much up for just getting out of the helicopter anywhere.

Jim also reflected also that the secondary DOP was actually very much along the lines of his preferred start position, the one he wanted to be in when initially planning the mission back in Hereford. Albeit that the approach was from the east rather than the west. The others in the patrol took the same view as Jim that whilst not ideal, the secondary DOP was the best balance for avoiding capture and still having the opportunity to complete at least in part the mission. Vic had already started planning ahead thinking about steal a vehicle to get us back into range of the target. Great fighting spirit, reflected Jim, feels a bit like "Where Eagles Dare" in our case we don't know where the aircraft or pilots are located.

"If circumstances arise do you think you can make the secondary DOP?" Jim asked Jeff.

"It will depend on visibility," said Jeff we don't know much about the border region.

"We do our best," he continued.

"Then that's all we can ask for." said Jim.

"Will has detection equipment that can show whether we are being illuminated on enemy radar." Jeff continued his briefing.

"If this happens we execute a banking manoeuvre and Roy completes the countermeasures." Jeff paused.

"What does that mean." asked Ed.

"Well we release reflective materials, sort of like buckets of silver paper, from the back of the helicopter." Jeff continued "this helps prevent the enemy radar systems getting a missile lock."

Jim looked around the room; no one said anything but he could tell what they were thinking, "fuck me, buckets of silver paper to divert missile attack, just something that happens all the time!"

Jeff looked around the room and then continued. "After drop off we fly west into Chile and attempt to ditch the helicopter into the sea. Our goal is to avoid detection for as long as possible. If news of the ditched helicopter gets out the whole of Argentinian Tierra del Fuego will be heaving with enemy forces looking for you. I hope we can hold off for 3-4 days at least then our orders are to surrender to Chilean Authorities. The cover story is that we were on a routine patrol and got lost in bad weather." He smiled knowingly at the team. "Of course they will be bound to believe us!"

"In that case met permitting we plan to take off at 0015hrs, so we need to be ready to move onto the deck at 2345hrs."

There were no further questions and the teams went off in search of tea and if possible a late lunch.

During the rest of the afternoon the team checked their equipment, for the final time. Jim decided on whether there was anything he could leave to lighten the load a little. They had distributed ammunition, explosives and timing devices more or less evenly. Nick was carrying the radio, a fairly heavy and bulky item so they also distributed his additional kit round the patrol as best they could. Now it was time for some rest before the Operation. The patrol had been allocated some space in a corridor area; they reasoned that it was well down in the vessel, maybe under the waterline. So here they were lying on top of their sleeping bags trying to sleep.

Jim wasn't sure how the others felt but he definitely had a knotted stomach and felt slightly clammy. The atmosphere was a bit hot and oppressive anyway and he noticed that his sweat was thick and sticky.

Over a bite to eat earlier he had met up with a Paul senior NCO he knew quite well. Prior to deployment he told Jim he had been on lengthy trip to US (Delta Force) immediately on return to Hereford his Squadron were deploying to the South Atlantic so he just grabbed his kit and went off with the others without getting the chance to say hullo and goodbye to his wife and small child. He seemed to be feeling a bit bad about this as he explained to Jim he had only recently realized just how hard it was for his wife when in earlier days he was totally absorbed by the regiment.

Jim lay in a kind of stupor, was this a true moment of destiny? Right now he wasn't so sure. Privately it felt more like a poison chalice, not that he felt bitter about being the chosen for the mission, someone had to go and in many ways it was an honour to have been selected for the mission. Also the options for the rest of his Squadron weren't that hot. If anything it was the sense of, in his opinion, misplaced optimism and expectation that made him feel quite guilty. In such circumstances it would have been good to feel some strong belief in success and that the odds could be a little more stacked in their favour. Just getting to the target area was dramatic enough; then God knows what they might find. He thought about his family, working on the farm, old girlfriends, playing rugby with his mates and having a few beers afterwards. A life of drama and excitement was great but you really needed a sense of perspective. Drifting in and out of slumber, his mind buzzing, he really was physically dog tired. He promised himself that never again would he turn his nose up at the simple pleasures. Mind you he had some good times in the Regiment as in his drowsy state he recalled some of the events of the previous 3 years.

Chapter 10

Central America 1981

First light and the patrol were ready to move, they were on hard routine so it was sleeping on the deck. The good thing about the jungle was you generally managed to get a good night's sleep. At least once you had let go of the fear of things that crawl, wriggle and bite. Darkness fell suddenly and totally at around 1800hrs and it didn't get light until around 0600hrs the following day. As it was pitch black and impossible to move around it wasn't generally necessary to post sentries, well at least while you were submerged in dense jungle. At times it was so thick that if you just walked away into the undergrowth for a piss or a crap you could get lost. Jim had thought that this had sounded totally crazy when it had had been explained during continuation training but had soon found out for himself that it was true. No secrets in this place you needed to have line of sight to your mates.

There were 8 in the patrol moving slowly now through thick secondary jungle. Apparently the really big trees had been logged in the 1920s. Still there were some monsters growing, huge trunks with winged roots projecting from the base of the trunk. Going was hard and their jungle uniforms were always soaked in sweat. Always wet or at least damp and if it's not rain it's sweat, thought Jim. Their packs weighed around 70lb and each man carried an Armalite M16 rifle with about 200 rounds and backup 9mm Browning pistol. The packs were made heavier by that need for each man to carry 1 gallon of water. Despite plenty of rain, finding surface water could be difficult in the jungle; apparently it was to do with the limestone rocks and thin subsoil. They were wearing US issue boots and uniforms which were effectively non attributable there being such a proliferation of ex US service kit in the world. Communicating using arm signals and occasionally in whispers they made their way to the RV which was about 400m short of the target. It was now late morning and so they fortified themselves with tinned cheese and biscuits and a few sips of water.

Jim and Ed went forward to perform a reconnaissance of the best site for the ambush. About 2 hours later they returned to the RV. There was just time to deliver quick patrol orders, then to send a Sitrep signal back to base, and to grab a cold snack before they moved into ambush position. Jim needed to get everything set up before darkness. About 90 minutes later they were in ambush position round the track known to be used by the enemy forces. Initiation of the ambush would be the electronic detonation of a Claymore mine. This had been carefully sited to ensure that it fired down the track into the advancing enemy forces. Jim recalled his instructor's words, "the Claymore mine fires 700 steel balls in a horizontal 60° fan-shaped arc that is 2 meters high and 50 meters wide, these are propelled by a shaped 3.5lb explosive charge, potentially lethal out to 100m and it can really fuck up your whole day."

They had split the patrol, 2 cut offs, of 2 men at each end of the ambush zone with 4 men including Jim in the centre. Once the Claymore was detonated it was a clear signal to open fire. Darkness fell quickly; there was a sense of anticipation that as soon as it got light there might be some action. The men made themselves as comfortable as possible and prepared to wait in position so they would be ready at first light.

First light, Jim shook himself and rubbed his eyes, he looked across to Ed who gave him the thumbs up. Looking around he could see the others and could also gently feel the tugging on the communications line. Definitely footsteps, low voices and people walking down the track towards them. As ever that feeling of excitement, just like he had felt when his grandfather had taught him to shoot all those years ago on the farm. Fingers now ready on the wires, one already in the battery and the other ready to make contact for detonation.

Counting 3 maybe 4 people moving along the track, from the intelligence this was likely to be all. He could make out the outline of the Armalite rifles they carried. First one through past the claymore, easy does it, now thought Jim, pressing the wire into the battery. There was a loud explosion followed by the crack of high velocity rifle firing, then all quiet, the smell of explosives and burning, smoke lingering in the trees. Targets will fall when hit. Mission accomplished so time to bug out to the pick-up point before someone comes looking for us.

Chapter 11

Oman 1981

The sun beat down on the old dhow as they rounded the Strait of Hormuz. To the North you could see the coastline of Iran, huge brown jelly fish floated in the dark waters round the Musandam Peninsular. The deck smelt of salt and slightly rotting fish guts, probably from the tuna they had landed yesterday. Jim was amazed at how the sea just instantly became very deep away from the rocky coastline. Snapper, Pete and Tommie made up the rest of the patrol, along with 4 members of the Sultan's Armed Forces (SAF). Their mission, which to date had been uneventful and great fun was to patrol the Northern coastline of Oman, delivering hearts and minds support into the coastal communities before returning to the Omani Naval Base at Goat Island. They had been briefed that there were pirates operating in the area so there was always the added possibility of just a little excitement. If they were attacked it was open hunting season.

So far life had been pretty uneventful. The previous evening they had eaten fresh tuna which had been caught from the dhow earlier that day and then slept on a beach. All good stuff, the only slightly disconcerting part was the youngest SAF soldier appeared to take a shine him. Tommie had subsequently compounded the problem by having a conversation in Arabic that Jim didn't understand but had subsequently explained with broad grin "Boss, he says tonight he wants to sleep with the English captain."

Jim was pretty sure that Tommie was winding him up, much to everyone's amusement. But all the same he had still slept on his green maggot with his 9mm Browning across his chest, one round up the spout, just in case. In the cold light of day this probably wasn't so smart, "what if I had dreamt of removing the safety catch?" He pondered.

That evening Snapper was telling some war stories round the fire, he was a veteran of the war in Oman and in particular the battle of Mirbat. Jim reflected on the first time he had met Snapper, just after passing selection. It was in a Hereford wine bar, Snapper had walked up and introduced himself. Jim had been slightly overalled, Snapper was quite heavily built and about 6 feet tall with brown hair, dark but hollow staring eyes, and he had a loud voice and forthright nature. "Ah Boss so you are going to join my Troop, I followed your progress on officer's week." he had said. Jim liked him although he did wonder whether the rest of the troop who had yet to meet was going to be full of snapper lookalikes.

Jim had also discovered that Snapper had fairly recently retaken selection after being banished to the Royal Engineers for a year, following what Snapper himself had described as 'a bit of drama' whilst working on a training advisory task in the Far East. During a break one drink had led to another and there had been a scrap with some of the locals, with the inevitable consequences, damage to a bar and several locals had been hospitalised. When the police arrived to make things worst Snapper had decided 'he didn't want to be arrested' which had made things even worst. Eventually when lots of police arrived he wound up in a prison cell and early the following morning had appeared in front of a local magistrate. This was before anyone from the Embassy could help out. The alternatives available were 1 month in a local prison or 6 strokes of the cane. Being a hard bastard he opted for the cane, as he pointed out living in a local prison could have been far worst, the water was filthy, prisoners ate cockroaches and he didn't know whether the local diplomats would be able to get him out anyway.

Snapper described how he had been immediately taken form the court room, stripped bollock naked and tied face down across a bamboo frame, which he subsequently described as 'the apparatus'. Next enter what seemed to be a man wearing only Kung Fu style trousers and wielding a swishy bamboo composite cane to administer the punishment. Snapper said he could only remember the first blow; it had hurt so much, and then thinking that he had probably made the worst mistake of his life. What followed was something of a blur. Being collected and delivered to the airport in a wheelchair, unable to walk for a few days. On his return to Hereford he was banished from the SAS and worked at the RE recruitment depot for a year until he could retake selection. Having regaled everyone with the story, to much amusement and cries of "tell us about the apparatus" he said you know boss, "wherever I go drama seems really seems to follow me like a plague."

Later that day the relative peace of the patrol was indeed disturbed by a small moment of perhaps not high but at least drama. Snapper explained to the SAF soldiers that we planned to visit a small village on the east coast, for some unknown reason this created a bit of a stir and their commander, a Corporal, became very animated and angry. He explained that this was not possible and could never happen. At least that was the translated version Jim had picked up from Snapper. FN Rifles belonging to the SAF patrol members waved first in the in the air and then more in Jim and Snapper's direction. Jim and Snapper already had cocked weapons, SLR rifles and 9mm pistols, so without pointing these around too much to inflame the situation they tried to be ready just in case. There was a stand-off, not unlike the shoot-out at the OK Corral Jim was later to reflect. Probably very bad for the career to get into a gun fight with friendly forces but on the other hand as Snapper was quick to point out always better to be judged by 12 rather than carried by 6.

Each party kept their distance and when the situation had calmed a little Jim remembered that the SAF commander for the Musandam was a former colleague from his School of Infantry Course at Warminster. They managed to get him on the radio and explained the situation. The SAF Corporal had then been summoned to the radio; somewhat grudgingly he appeared and took the handset disbelievingly. Jim would never forget the look on his face as he stiffened and stood to attention whilst holding the handset. The boys were trying to supress grins. Good to maintain contacts reflected Jim. "Boss I told you that drama follows me like a plague," Snapper reminded him.

Chapter 12

Insertion May 1982

Jim woke from his rest with a start, no Snapper although there was some drama in the air. An "Action Stations" was called as a result of air raid warnings. Jim and the patrol moved to an assembly point through the steel bulkhead doors and just sit there looking at each other, trying to smile and wondering what next. They are joined by 10 or more sailors wearing white flash hoods and gloves. As they had arrived in a somewhat unorthodox manner Jim and his team did not have this equipment, not that it was likely to make too much difference anyway Jim reasoned. There really is nothing to do but hope that the Argies miss. As far as Jim was aware and solely based on the principle of no loud bangs or shocks, no bombs have landed near Invincible. Eventually there was a call over the intercom ending the Action Stations, "thank fuck for that, Boss," murmured Ed. "It's hard not knowing what's going on, feels like a large steel coffin, not that I really know what that feels like he added quickly."

"I don't fancy their job much, Ed" said Jim, as they moved back through a series of steel doors. "I wouldn't want to be stuck on the wrong side of one of these doors."

"Probably a mutual feeling then," said Ed. "I'm not sure there are many people who fancy their chances of success in our little show either."

"I think the worst aspect is having no control over your own destiny," added Jim. "Applicable to us all I think." He added with a wry smile.

They moved off with the others to the senior ratings mess where they were provided with a huge steak meal. This was a special provided by a sailor who seemed to know where they were heading.

"You know Boss I can almost see the love in that Guys eyes," said Mike.

Not having much of an appetite Jim still did his best to polish off the meal. The others did the same. There was a general feeling of calm and goodwill between everyone. "Sort of feels a bit like the condemned men ate a hearty meal." Tom tried to joke.

"What would you be doing back in Hereford now Vic?" asked Rob. "Well before all this, I'd just met the fittest bird, seriously hot, gets turned on just by being in my company. Wears full webbing. Last time we went out she was so hot that she wanted it in the pub car park before we got back to her place."

"Bollocks," said Rob. It made everyone smile.

Vic continued, "well now this little job and the build up to it, has slightly messed up my personal life. Can't wait to get back, I'll be even more irresistible"

"Listen to him, here we are just about to fly off into the unknown and all he can think about is sex." Rob smiled.

They thanked the sailor for the meal shake hands and move back to the briefing area to make a final check on the kit.

Ian asked "How long before we go Boss?"

"Need to be ready to move onto the deck in about 2 hours," replied Jim.

"Just time to check over the kit and go through our actions on being dropped off," Ed nodded. "Maybe we can do that over a final brew?"

At 2330hrs Jim and the other 7 patrol members were guided onto the flight deck. Their bergens were well stuffed and heavy. It felt cold and windy but much fresher after the somewhat clammy heat down below. It was very dark, probably cloudy as no starts were visible. In the dim light on deck everything seemed uniformly dark grey. They moved towards the silhouette of the Sea King and met up with Jeff, Will and Roy.

"Roy will load you into the aircraft and take you through the necessary drills. It's not going to be a very comfortable ride as we've stripped out any unnecessary equipment to save weight." Jeff added. "I'm going to get things set up with Will. When you are all loaded come forward and I can give you the low down." With that he and Will climbed into the cockpit.

Roy helped the patrol load their kit into the helicopter, which true to form had been stripped bare.

"Probably best if you all wear these," Roy handed out florescent orange immersion suits. "It might help if we get a problem on take-off," Roy added.

Jim and the others pulled the suits on over their uniforms, they felt clumsy and awkward.

"Not sure what these will do for us if there is a drama, Boss" said Vic.

"It'll keep us warm on the trip if nothing else," said Ed.

"Best remember to take them off before we reach the target or the Argies will see us in the dark," he continued.

Under Roy's direction they climbed aboard and loaded their equipment down the centre trying to keep the weight distribution fairly even then and sat on the floor, 4 each side leaning against the fuselage. It felt dark and cold to Jim, the floor was hard but he supposed that was the least of his worries.

Whilst climbing aboard Jim noticed several buckets of what looked like pieces of silver paper. He realised that this must be the 'chaff' to be used as a counter measure should they be locked by enemy radar. He sincerely hoped that it would not be required.

Jeff turned and gave the thumbs up. The engine started and they waited until he was ready for the take-off. He was waiting for the carrier to reach maximum speed into the wind to assist in giving more lift. Everyone knew this was a critical time, falling off the back of the carrier and ditching into the sea would be a very bad option immersion suit or not. This baby isn't going to float. Jim could feel the tension, it was too noisy for anyone to speak, in the occasional flash of light he could see the tension in the face of Nick who was sitting opposite.

Jim glanced at his watch it was just after midnight, date showing as 18 May. The noise of the engine rose slowly as they seemed to just lift off the deck. There was one heart stopping moment as they felt like they were dropping towards the sea before Jeff took control and they became stable and are away, flying at what seemed to be a few feet above the waves. Jim managed to smile through gritted teeth, thinking well that's one part of this horror show down, more to come, probably much worse but at least they won't be needing to do that again.

It was very dark, there was a low level of light from the instrument panel, but Jim could just make out the silhouettes of the others. The good news was that the smell of aviation fuel that had plagued previous flights was missing. No colours in the darkness except for some dim lights on the instrument panel in the cockpit.

The noise made it impossible to speak; Jim wondered what the others were thinking. He tried to focus on the task ahead but the level of uncertainty made it very hard. What would the ground be like, were there significant enemy forces in the vicinity, he hoped not, would they even fucking well get there? He fervently hoped they would! Jim reflected that it was always harder when things moved totally out of control. Best to just take things as they come, not quite 'thumb up bum and mind in neutral', as his old Sandhurst Instructor used to joke when someone wasn't paying attention, but well for the next 3-4 hours and 300 plus nautical miles all you could really do was to sit back and enjoy the ride.

Slowly the helicopter skimmed over the waves westwards towards the Argentinian coastline.

Chapter 13

Insertion

The trip so far had been uneventful, about 3 hours so far Jim thought as he looked at his watch. Despite having the opportunity to snatch an hour or two's sleep it wasn't easy in the back of the stripped out Sea King. Jim still felt slightly weary and his mouth was dry. His ears rang he moved forwards towards the cockpit. He could make out the silhouettes of Jeff to his right and Will to the left. Will passed him a headset so that he was in direct contact. Magic he thought, as much of the engine noise was cut out.

As they approach the coastline there is a powerful red glow to the west. To Jim, after the hours of relative darkness it seemed to burn with great intensity almost hurting his eyes. He was curious to understand what it might be. The glow seemed to get brighter and brighter filling the sky; it was hard to judge the distance and they passes through the glow the source of which seemed to come from the starboard side.

"Must be an oil rig," said Will.

"Imagine they must have radar, we have changed course a little to attempt to avoid detection."

He sounded confident to Jim, who was completely unaware that there was an offshore drilling operation off the Argentinian coast of Tierra del Fuego.

The glow slowly faded and after about 10 minutes he could make out the silhouette of the approaching coast line.

"Here we go," said Jeff.

Looking down Jim could see what looked like a lighthouse.

"We will use this as a reference point to set up our navigation system," he said.

Both Jeff and Will donned Passive Night Goggles (PNG), "we'll need to keep very low to avoid ground radars and so will be flying very slowly," Jeff added. "These little babies help us to see in the dark."

As they moved inland visibility became very poor indeed. There was thick fog and as far as Jim was concerned he certainly couldn't see anything through the windshield. Maybe just as well he thought.

Will was busy using a device that helped determine whether they were being illuminated by enemy radar. They moved very slowly and Jim couldn't help wondering if they were flying so low how much noise they might be making to any locals and ground forces. Difficult conditions to just go in and out, so unfortunately there would be much surprise, he considered the impact. He hoped that there would not be a welcoming party. In his mind he had imagined a fast in and out, this didn't seem to be working out.

If anything the visibility was getting worse and they seemed to be in the air for ages. It was hard to say exactly how long as he felt worried and a little tense.

"About 5 minutes to go now," warned Jeff.

Will showed him their approximate position on the map.

Jim knew the aircrew had done there very best to get him and his team into position. Right now with all the low level flying, what felt like the helicopter changing directions, fog and concern over enemy radar, if you had put him on the rack he would maybe have confessed to not being 100% confident on their position. That was not to say there was any hard data whatsoever to base this judgement on just a feeling; he recalled lots of horror stories about patrols being accidentally dropped off in the wrong place.

No withstanding this reservation Jim went back and gave the thumbs up to Ed and raised his fingers indicating 5 minutes.

Ed nodded and passed the signal on; the helicopter was moving around a bit, not really flying in a straight line. It was hard for the team to keep their balance and move the kit ready for exit.

Jim moved back to the front. His eyes scanned right and left into the gloom.

Looking out to his right he saw what he thought were lights flashing through the mist.

At the same time Jeff continued his descent hovering over the drop off point.

Jim looked out to where he had seen lights, there was darkness and then a flash of light into the sky, visibility very poor but as far as Jim was concerned it looked like a flare. Given the fog it was hard to judge the distance. After all the noise what if they had been tracked and there really was a welcoming party on the ground?

Fuck what a horrible position, he cursed. His decision probably took only a few seconds but it felt like an age. Standard procedure for the patrol would be to abort this position and try at the alternative DOP, some way to the west and near to the border. There had been heavy political overtones on this job so it really needed to be balanced against the huge weight of expectation, the extraordinary lengths that so many people had gone to get them into this position. Jim didn't want to be the 'Rupert' not to lead his men out of the helicopter equally he didn't want to be the one to lead them into immediate danger. He though "damned if you do and damned if you don't. Not much fucking use to anyone if I order everyone out here and we all get captured before we have the chance to do anything, a no win situation all round."

Decision made then, he told Jeff. At the end of the day it was Jim the patrol commander's responsibility to judge whether the DOP had been compromised.

"I'm not happy; it doesn't feel right, it seems entirely possible to me that the DOP has been compromised." Continuing, "I want to move to the alternative RV, we are not getting out here."

Stunned silence from Jeff, who having worked so hard to get Jim and his men into position may not have totally understood the rationale for Jim's decision; all the same he realised there was no point in hanging around.

Jim was slightly taken back; he thought perhaps Jeff just didn't see the lights and what looked like the flare?

"OK," Jeff eventually gulped, continuing "bad visibility means it's not going to be easy getting you to the secondary DOP, we can try."

Jim moved back, tapped Ed and quickly gave him the new instruction, practically shouting in his ear against the background noise.

"Possible compromise, Secondary DOP, near Chile border," he shouted.

The 7 men in the patrol were in position ready to jump the last few feet out of the back of the hovering Sea King. As the instruction filtered down the line they immediately stopped what they were doing and shuffled with their kit back into the helicopter

Tom who had been first in line was already out the back and needed to be helped back in.

"Fucking hell, I thought you bastards were going to leave me there on my own!" he had remarked later when things had quietened down.

The decision made the helicopter continued on the low level path flying slowly westwards. To Jim progress seemed painfully slow. He realised that Jeff and his team were finding the low level flying in the fog very difficult. Ten minutes or so later they came very close to disaster. Suddenly a dark shape loomed directly ahead out of the fog. Jim took it to be the side of a hillside.

In an instant Jeff banked sharply to the starboard and the obstacle flashed past on the port side.

Strangely everything happened in slow motion. "You know they say your life flashes before you, well it is true," thought Jim, "fuck me that felt close."

Apart from the sharp banking he guessed the boys in the back would not know anything of the drama or just how close they may have come to piling in.

The near miss precipitates a conversation between Jeff and Will. The situation is tense but they still remain calm and matter of fact. This impresses Jim.

"The visibility is certainly not getting any better, Will," said Jeff.

"I reckon we may need to gain height, we can't really avoid this happening again and may not be so lucky next time."

Will agreed but pointed out that but climbing higher they ran a risk of being detected by radar and potentially being the target for ground to air missiles.

"Risky," he said "but I agree in the circumstances there doesn't seem much else we can do."

"Jim once we gain height there's no guarantee we'll be able to come down anywhere near the secondary DOP as planned. The only way will be find the sea and work our way inland again. We are also running low on fuel."

"I don't see we have any choice, this isn't going to work. Just get us as near to the border as you reasonably can," agreed Jim.

Decision made, Jeff gained height rising to about 2000ft, this lifted the helicopter above the layer of mist and poor visibility and headed westwards at top speed. Some relief but this was short lived. The increased altitude may have reduced the risk of piling in but it soon brought other problems.

"We are being detected by their radar; they have a lock on our position." Will was holding a radar detection device.

Jim reflected, "This is not a nice feeling, I wonder if you know anything about being blown out of the sky at 2000 feet. Probably not he reasoned. So nothing to do but pray to your maker for a reprieve, wait and hope for the best then."

In response to the missile threat Jeff decided to initiate countermeasures.

He passed his instructions to Roy, seconds later the helicopter banked steeply and although Jim could not see what was going on at the back he imagined Roy throwing the buckets of chaff out of the starboard door. This process was repeated.

Things moved slowly back on an even keel, Will seemed less bothered about radar detection. Although from time to time he indicated they were being detected by radar.

Jeff held course and after about 15 minutes he announced they were in Chilean airspace having crossed the border.

"We can't run the risk of trying to land through this mist, I just don't know what's down there," he said.

Mixed feelings then, Jim felt an obvious sense of relief that they were unlikely to be shot down but realised from a mission perspective things had deteriorated even further. In fact they would be in the shit albeit from a different perspective. Far from being dropped off at the secondary DOP they were flying deeper into Chile. This would make their task even harder more than likely impossible.

After another 10 minutes of flying, Jim presumed westwards they reached the sea and visibility improved. He could make out the coastline below.

Jeff flew over the sea; following their pre-arranged drill the aircrew 9mm pistols were collected by Roy and thrown into the sea. The helicopter turned and approached the land from what Jim assumed would now be the west.

"We have to ditch this baby away from here and are running pretty low on fuel. I'll do what I can to get you inland as far as I can but the visibility is still poor."

"OK whatever you can do will help," said Jim.

Jim went back to shout the warning order they were about to land into Ed's ear.

The helicopter flew back inland, after about 5 minutes Jeff said "This is it; we will put you down now."

The helicopter hovered over what looked to be a reasonably flat and featureless area.

As best he could Will showed Jim their location.

"I reckon we are about here, he indicated the position on his map."

Jim took a good look; it was hard to see in the dim light.

He memorised it, "best of luck guys," hoping he could translate it onto his map.

"Fuck this has really gone tits up; we are a hell of a way from the border, let alone Rio Grande" There was a kind of sinking feeling in his stomach, not just a legacy of the fear of being shot down, whilst he didn't consider he was to blame for their position nonetheless here they all were, looking on the bright side seemingly safe and well and nowhere near their objective. Jim was thinking ahead "I'm not too sure how the powers that be, will take this." He gritted his teeth, well they weren't fucking well here, and they hadn't just been through the ride from hell, so time to move on."

He quickly shook hands with Jeff and Will removed the headset and departed out of the back. He tapped Roy on the shoulder, shouted thanks and followed the rest of the patrol out of the rear starboard door into the darkness.

Chapter 14

Chile

The patrol had dismounted with their equipment and moved into a rough circle. They adopted fire positions in the event that the helicopter had attracted any unwelcome attention. Mind you it would be tricky getting involved in a shoot-out with the Chilean authorities, definitely one to avoid Jim reflected. He hoped that they had landed unnoticed. The helicopter disappeared off to the west. After a few minutes he realised that for the time being any form of compromise was highly unlikely. It was pitch black, freezing cold and as far as he could tell they were in the middle of nowhere. The ground below felt wet and a bit marshy. The strong south westerly wind had picked up, the mist and fog completely gone and the wind was blowing sleet and rain into his eyes. "Welcome to Tierra del Fuego, what a miserable place," he thought.

Jim nudged Ed who passed on the signal and they moved closer together, keeping low to the ground they huddled together close enough for Jim to explain at least in outline, the possible compromise, the problems flying with poor visibility and radar detection. He then moved onto what he believed to be their current location. He pointed to the location on the map, "this is where Will thinks we are," he said. In the dim light of the torch on the black and white map they could see they were to the south and east of a bay shown as 'Bahia Inutil'; inland about 10 km and so maybe 20-30 km from the border. As Rio Grande was just a black dot on the other side of the map and there was nothing to show where the airfield was located. As far as they could tell from the border there would be another 25 km or so to airfield. "So just 50 km or so adrift," then he reflected.

"Helpful map, Boss" said Ian echoing the views of everyone, "I can see an outline of the coast, a line for the border, and lines for a couple of rivers, a few Spanish names and a fucking dot for Rio Grande. There isn't much to tell us what it's like in between."

"Ok so we need to do our best to confirm the location when it gets light. In the meantime we should walk east and get as far as possible towards the border before it gets light. If we can find a suitable lie up position LUP before it gets light we should be in good shape to try and establish radio communications. We need to avoid contact with any locals at all costs but we don't treat them like enemy forces remember we are in Chile. Let's not make anything worst. Everyone agree?"

No one complained, realising they were in the shit but perhaps not much as in the shit as they could have been, so stoic responses all round. As no one appeared to have a better suggestion they quickly picked up their equipment and moved off, as previously agreed, in single file. The 80lb Bergen felt heavy on Jim's back. Mike was leading the way, his welrod at the ready, heading off on an easterly bearing. The wind had picked up and now was at their back blowing cold and strong. The sleet had turned to snow and was beginning to lie on the ground, merging with the patched of wet snow left over from some earlier fall. The going was quite difficult; rough but not rocky. There were small hills with large tufts of 'moon grass' and boggy patches in the lower areas. Not much vegetation to be seen, in fact to Jim it was very reminiscent of the ground they had all encountered during selection in the Elan Valley of Central Wales. No surprises then that their progress was quite slow.

After an hour they stopped for 5 minutes, circled round and listen. Filthy weather, strong wind, it's as bleak as fuck, reckon you would be pretty unlikely to meet anyone out here, thought Jim.

He estimated that they had maybe covered 3 km and it was about 0500hrs local time, probably another 2 hours until it started to get light. After 5 minutes they move off, slowly progressing eastwards. The snow was blowing in on the cold wind at their back. Despite the cold Jim was sweating inside his windproof smock. They continued for maybe another 2 km before stopping.

"Right we need to find somewhere with some cover, before it gets light." Jim whispered.

"Mike and Ian take a quick look round, don't be too long or we'll all die of exposure." He added.

After about 10 minutes they returned.

"Found a good location just over the brow, nearby running water with some cover, also it might help keep off the wind." Mike said.

"All mod cons then," said Ed.

Jim felt stiff and cold as he pulled himself to his feet. No doubt the others felt much the same. On reflection though, still they lived and were ready to fight another day.

The fast flowing stream was shallow; whilst it was cold it wasn't cold enough to freeze the running water, just about zero Celsius maybe a degree or so lower thought Jim. They spread out in the cover of the gorse like bushes. Prior to leaving Hereford some thoughtful person had carried out a raid on the local Cotswold camping store. So they had all been given goretex jackets, hollow fill sleeping bags and also lightweight one man tents. Whilst the kit was hardly tried and tested some of it was useful. After some thought Jim decided that despite the weight he would bring the jacket, he could always dump it if it became a liability. There was no room for the tent poles but the tent would suffice as a cover for his sleeping bag. In addition there was no way he was going to leave the green maggot behind as this was truly tried and tested and worked even when wet. Therefore he dumped the lightweight hollow fill sleeping bag.

When he stopped he put the goretex jacket over his SAS smock, it proved to be a real life saver. Jim used the lightweight tent as an exterior cover for his sleeping bag. This wasn't ideal as his sleeping bag quickly became wet where it touched the cover. Still better than nothing he thought at least another layer of insulation. They agreed to a 30 minute sentry roster which would give them the opportunity to get a few hours rest each and amidst the falling snow tried to get warm in their sleeping bags.

Jim awoke to about 6" of wet snow on top of his one man tent. He was warm and fairly dry but the inside of the tent was soaking and as a result his sleeping bag was also wet. He pulled himself up and quickly rolled up his kit and stuffed it away. They were in the cover of the gorse like bushes and he could hear the noise of the running water from the stream. He looked around and whilst Ed was on sentry duty a little way down the hill at the edge of the thicket. The others were stowing their kit and making a brew.

"Seems quiet, Boss" said Ian in a low voice. "Filthy climate, I can't imagine there are too many people living here." He added.

"Strangely I think it was populated largely by the Welsh and Scots, good for sheep farming as I understand it." Nick chipped in.

"Get fucking everywhere, they do," said Ian. "Can you imagine wanting to live here?"

"Anyone seen Vic?" Asked Jim,

"Checked him earlier, Boss" said Ian, "he's not feeling so good.

Jim moved across to the one man tent, Vic was lying inside. He could see Vic was shivering and looked pretty pale. "How are you feeling?" He asked

"I'm feeling pretty weak; think I've got a temperature and my throats sore like I've got some sort of infection. I made a mistake bringing this hollow fill sleeping bag. It's completely soaked and fucking useless. It was wet before we started"

Tom who was the patrol medic moved across.

"Hey mate we need to get you as warm and dry as possible. Have you got anything dry?"

Vic struggled out of his one man tent and bag. Ian went through Vic's Bergen and found a dryish jumper. Fortunately it had stopped snowing, there was still a brisk wind but if anything it felt a little warmer.

"Thanks," said Vic removing his smock and pulling on the jumper. He put his smock back on top and one of the boys gave him a brew.

"Take these," said Tom. He handed Vic two painkillers.

"We are going to stay here for a bit, in fact in an hour, 1100hrs local time we will need to test out the satellite communications with Hereford. Definitely no move before nightfall and then we'll see how you feel." Jim added.

"Briefing Hereford on this isn't going to be much fun," reflected Jim. Unless you had been on the helicopter understanding just how far they were from their objective was not going to be an easy one to explain.

Nick was working in the background to get the communications established. It was important to get the dish pointed at the correct angle ready for the satellite to pass overhead at the appointed hour.

"Looks like it's working ok Boss," said Nick.

He passed the headset to Jim.

Jim took a deep breath, they had been briefed that the communication line was completely secure so they could speak normally.

He recognised the friendly voice at the other end of the line. It was Vince a former RSM who was working in the CRW team.

Having quickly explained the details of the aborted insertion and how they now found themselves some distance from the target, Jim explained that they intended to try and pin point their location, lie up for the rest of the daylight hours and then if Vic was up to it move further towards the border.

Vince was a hard headed character, "sounds like you are out of it at least for a bit Jim, and we may need to work out how to extract you ready for redeployment. I'll brief Group on what has happened and I'll give you an update at the pre-arranged time tomorrow."

Whilst Jim was on the radio, Ed and Ian had been doing their best to work out the location. This wasn't easy as the ground was pretty much featureless and anyway there wasn't much on the map to orientate against. Using the assumption that the drop off location had been correct and they had covered about 5 km during their night march. They calculated maybe 15 km to the border and another 25 km to the airfield.

"OK so if the going improved, allowing for moving only at night, it would take us maybe 2-3 days to get anywhere near to the airfield," said Jim.

"Maybe longer, Boss," said Ed.

"Don't forget once we are in Argentina we will need to move more cautiously, it could take us twice as long."

"We've all got about 3 days rations left, not looking so good then" Jim observed.

"Probably best to wait and see how Vic is and we can decide what to do later." He added.

Possible options were running through his mind. He discussed them with the patrol. First option do they split up the patrol, perhaps leaving 1 or 2 with Vic?

Alternatively staying together to see how quickly Vic got better, if they couldn't make it across the border at least getting picked up and then perhaps redeployed.

Ed favoured staying together; in fact this was the general consensus. "I can Park the decision until tonight anyway," reflected Jim.

The day passed uneventfully in the lie up position, it was cold maybe just above freezing, and the snow had turned a little slushy. We really are in the middle of nowhere thought Jim.

Vic said he was feeling a little better not well enough the march but give it another day and maybe he would be well enough to continue. Decision made then, "we remain here for another 24 hours, then we can continue towards the border" he informed the patrol. Mixed feelings everyone happy that Vic appears to be on the mend whilst the underlying feeling that they are not being much assistance in the war effort, stuck in the middle of Tierra del Fuego miles from anywhere.

The wind had dropped and the sky had cleared, "reckon it will freeze tonight," said Ed. In fact the snow had already turned crunchy.

Later that night, Jim lay awake looking up at the stars. There was ice on top of his one man tent cover but it wasn't the cold that was bothering him. The situation they found themselves in meant it was increasingly unlikely they would ever be able to attempt their mission. His private view and he would only admit it if put on a rack first, was that the whole business had such a low chance of success and given the lack of target information it should not really have been attempted, at least in the current form. It had just a measure of how high the stakes had been and given there was still a war going on likely still were. Jim had felt that it was more than likely that the drop off had been compromised, the helicopter noise, lights, possible flare but given the high stakes had it been right for him to abort the DOP or should they have just got out anyway? Now here they were stuck in the middle of nowhere, no use to anyone and seemingly safely passing the war under a bush. Of course he wasn't to know that the weather conditions on the night of the insertion had meant that they had not been able to land at a secondary drop off nearer to the border. All the same he had made the decisions along the way and now here they were, not something he cared to discuss with the others and hard to explain but he had started to feel an overwhelming sense of guilt and maybe illogically failure. This superimposed on the current uncertainty was all together not a happy feeling.

The night passed without incident, as expected there was a heavy frost. The following morning Vic's condition had improved and they made plans to walk to the border as soon as it was dark.

During the morning signal call Jim had been asked to authenticate over the radio, as he discovered that

Hereford believed they had possibly been taken prisoner and were being forced to use the radio under duress.

"The Chilean authorities have found the helicopter and there are newspaper reports of 3,000 Argentinian troops looking for you along the border," was the headline update from Vince.

"We are making plans to extract you and you will be briefed tomorrow" he continued.

After the communication Jim discussed the position with the patrol.

"Maybe we give it one more go and move to the border?" asked Jim who wanted to solicit the views of the team.

"If we get to the border we can at least get some idea of the ground when we get redeployed," said Ed.

"Maybe we can steal some transport and still go the whole way," said Mike.

Jim felt that whilst this was an unlikely scenario he couldn't fault Mike for wanting to retrieve the mission.

"Ok let's give it our best shot, we'll move out as soon as it gets dark then," said Jim.

When it was dark they continued moving east, progress was slow, and a mixture of rain and sleet was blowing in on a strong south westerly wind.

It was very dark and there was no moon through the thick clouds. The going was rough in the rather featureless landscape. By daybreak Jim calculated they had maybe covered a further 15 km but were still probably 10 km short of the border. All completely knackered they moved into a lie up position in a small hollow surrounded by gorse. There was plenty of surface water and a small stream ran nearby.

"So not looking so good," then said Jim to Ed.

There was a cold wind blowing with light snow falling. Now it was colder the slush had gone crunchy and the falling snow had already started to fill in the green patches between lumps of lying snow.

"At this rate it will take us another day to reach the border." Replied Ed, he continued, "I don't know about you but I've got enough rations for about 2 days tops."

"About the same," replied Jim.

Although not wishing to admit defeat in front of Ed he added "I guess we are just too far away and will really need a resupply soon before we can continue eastwards."

The satellite communication has so far worked well, but this time Nick had some problems establishing communications. When they eventually got through to the friendly voice of Vince Jim explained their position.

"We are still maybe 10 km short of the border, highly unlikely we will be able to reach the target, given conditions on the ground."

"We want you to move to a pick up position; the RV will be open for 1 hour after dusk from tomorrow. The plan is to pull you out, get a resupply and then to work out the best way of redeploying you."

Vince went on to explain the position of the RV, which was a bridge over a river on the track running to the South of Bahia Inutil. Jim checked his map it was hard to be precise and pinpoint the RV as there were no grid references and the map just showed 4 unnamed rivers (lines) crossing the track. Their RV was to be the furthest west of these on the bridge over the river.

Hoping they had the right location Jim did a quick calculation. This would mean a trek back west north westwards of about 20 km.

"Yes, we can make this" he told Vince.

"Rod and his team will be there to collect you, best of luck." The radio went dead.

Everyone was pleased with the development.

"At least we won't be stuck here in limbo," said Vic.

"Wish we hadn't moved so far inland," said Ian, "mind you we know a bit more about the ground and we needed to find out just how feasible or otherwise it is to cover the ground on foot."

Spirits seemed to have lifter a little and everyone felt a renewed sense of purpose. Vic was feeling a lot better more like his old self.

Light snow fell during the rest of the morning, everything was grey, the horizon just blended into the ground. Later that afternoon the wind picked up and must have turned a little warmer although as it started to rain. What a filthy climate reflected Jim, rain, frost, snow in a never ending cycle.

As darkness fell there was a general mood of optimism. They moved off towards the RV. Jim knew it would be tough to make it to the RV, perhaps even to find it, apart from the lines on the map showing the position of the rivers against the track there were no features on the map that could be matched against the ground.

They marched through the night stopping for 10 minutes or so every hour. It was too cold and wet to stop for any longer although mercifully it had stopped raining, at about 2300hrs. The sky had cleared the wind dropped and the temperature had fallen so by the early hours there was a frost on the ground.

As best as Jim could determine they reached the area of the pick-up RV at about 0500 hrs. They needed to find a suitable lie up position in the vicinity and then to make a recce of the RV before it became light. Mike and Rob left their bergens and went off to find a suitable lie up position. They returned in about 20 minutes.

"The track is about 400m away and we have a position maybe 200m from here, Boss," said Mike. I reckon the RV is maybe 500m further in that direction, we should be able to locate it by keeping off the track if we can locate the river."

"OK thanks Mike," said Jim. "We'll move into position and then if you come with me we'll see if we can locate the RV."

The patrol moved to the lie up position. Mike and Jim went off to locate the RV. It was just starting to get light when they returned.

"How did it go?" asked Ed.

"We found the river, well more of a stream and the bridge over the road," said Mike.

"What's the road like?" Ed continued.

""Bit of a cart track, lots of potholes and loose stones," said Mike. "Good thing is there is no sign of any habitation or the locals."

"We went along the line of the track westwards for maybe another 500m or so," said Jim. "No sign of any other bridges so as far as we can tell this is the correct RV."

"Fucking well hope so," said Ed. "This is a miserable place."

"Could be much worst I suppose, we could be getting our arses shot off instead of sitting here under a bush having a brew," said Mike philosophically.

"Want the bad news Boss?" said Nick.

"Not really, but go ahead and make my day," said Jim.

"Radio is fucked, so we don't have any communications. To be honest I don't think there is anything I can do. It seemed a bit dodgy yesterday."

At times this might have been perceived as a blessing, no micro management or interference. However right now it constituted a bit of a problem.

"Fucking wonderful, I hope we are in the right place and we get picked up soon, otherwise we'll need a plan B before the rations run out. I think we are pretty friendly terms with Chile but to be honest I'd rather not find out." said Jim.

.

Chapter 15

Recovery

Just before last light Mike and Ian left the patrol position and moved to the RV just to one side of the bridge. There was a strong cold wind blowing from the south west but at least it was still dry. Jim and the others waited in the lie up position trying to keep warm, they couldn't hear or see anything as they were still too far from the track. As such they were very much hoping to receive the good news from Mike or Ian that they were ready to be picked up.

They waited and waited some more and nothing happened. "Not looking so good then Boss," said Ed between chattering teeth. "I'm glad I've still got my emergency rations!"

After about an hour Mike and Ian returned.

"Fuck me, I'm freezing," said the latter.

"Nothing moving on the track, quiet as a mouse. We waited for an extra 15 minutes," said Mike.

"Bollocks," said Jim.

"From all the information we have this looks to be the right place, maybe they had a problem, it can't be easy organising the logistics." He added, trying to sound optimistic.

"Nothing for it but to wait 24 hours," said Ed.

It was standard procedure never to leave the RV and to turn up 24 hours later if there was a no show.

A quick review of the status of their rations revealed that there was approximately 1 day left per man, so they agreed that the best approach was to make them last for 2 days.

Later that evening Jim lay in his sleeping bag looking up at the sky. Even though the drop off had in his opinion been compromised his decision to abort was really haunting him, now after a sequence of events here they all were in the middle of nowhere and miles from the action. A bit cold and hungry maybe but nonetheless seemingly out of danger. On reflection given the extraordinary lengths that everyone had gone to get them into this position and the weight of expectation, Jim was feeling huge guilt at there being no payback. He drifted in and out of sleep fitfully until it was his turn for sentry duty.

The wind had dropped during the night and with a clearing sky by morning there was a hard frost on the ground. Jim looked around at the white landscape. Feeling hungry he decided to eat half of his remaining porridge block dry, a couple of biscuits and some water. He decided to conserve his hexamine until later for a brew. Best to avoid using the plastic explosive as a substitute, who knows we may still need it. In an emergency it was possible to burn shavings of plastic explosive to provide a cooking fuel. Mind you use too much and you could burn right through your mess tin!

The early brightness soon passed and the clouds started piling in, later to add to the misery a mixture of cold rain and sleet started lashing in from the south west. Whilst there were no complaints everyone seemed subdued, each man buried in their own thoughts. Every available piece of kit was being worn in an attempt to keep warm. Jim was damp on the outside but his inner layer was still relatively warm and dry. There seemed little chance of compromise in their lie up position so they talked occasionally in low voices. Since the insertion they had been more or less cut off from the rest of the world and they were all concerned about the War and how it was going for the Task Force.

Later that afternoon the weather cleared and it became much colder with snow showers. Light snow was falling when Mike and Ian moved off to the RV just before last light.

"Now I know what it must be like living in the Shetland Islands," said Mike.

"More like bloody Iceland, I should think," said Ian.

Jim detected a slight air of optimism in the camp as the rest of them waited. Unfortunately this didn't last and after a seemingly endless hour they all knew that there would be no pick up tonight.

Mike and Ian returned, "some of you bastards can have a go tomorrow, it's fucking freezing waiting in this wind," said Mike.

"No one is coming because you smell so bad," said Rob.

They managed to smile.

"Seriously what do you reckon, Boss," asked Ian.

"Well as far as we can tell we are in the right place, I don't see much alternative than to stay put and give it one more go tomorrow. After that we may need to take matters into our own hands. Anyone else got a better plan?" Jim replied.

They all knew that basic training was never to leave the RV and for at least one more day that's what they would do. After this the rations would have definitely run out and they might need to think of a plan B.

Everyone was in agreement and so it was back to the same routine. Keep under cover and try to keep warm.

The next day was dry and cold. By last light everyone was down to emergency rations, "always knew the Mars bar would be useful" thought Jim, "I'll save it for tomorrow. At last light they tried a different pairing, so Ed and Rob moved off to the RV, just in case Mike and Ian were jinxed. This time there was an air of resignation in those that were left. It seemed hard to believe that the outcome would be any better than the previous 2 nights. Unfortunately they were correct in their analysis and Ed and Rob came back freezing cold and empty handed about 90 minutes later.

"What the fuck should we do now?" asked Ed.

"Given the shit we have for a map, as far as any of us can tell we are in the right place." He continued.

"Maybe we are in the right place, it's just that the team picking us up have run into some problems," said Mike.

"I think two of us should head into Porvenir and see if we can establish contact with the British Consul. If I can find a phone I've got the number in my notebook. They gave it to me before we left Hereford." Jim said.

"The remaining 6 can continue to man the RV, until we get assistance."

"Sounds reasonable who's going with you?" said Ed.

"I'll come Boss," said Nick, "it'll be good to get moving again."

"On this map it looks about 120 km round the coastal track, should be able to make it in 1-2 days then if the going is good, we can use the track under cover of darkness and take a view on using it when it gets light," said Jim.

"Might even have to take a lift if we can get one," said Nick. "It could take a while. If we leave the bulk of our equipment and rifles here," we'll be able to make better time. It might not attract so much attention if we bump into anyone," said Nick.

"Reckon we should keep our 9mm pistols, not sure exactly why but it makes me feel happier," said Jim.

The plan agreed they packed up their equipment ready to move with the others just in case in the event of a successful pick up.

Ten minutes later Jim and Nick were wished well by the remaining members of the patrol as they moved down towards the track.

"For fuck's sake remember to bring some fang back," was Ian's party shot.

To start with the wind was at their back and they moved fairly swiftly along the track. It felt good to be moving again. They reasoned that it was unlikely that they would meet anyone on foot in the middle of the night and if there was any traffic they would be able to pick up the headlights fairly soon and be able to move off the track.

After about 4 hours of steady walking, Jim said, "Nick what do you think? If we get the chance of bumming a lift, I think we should take it."

"Worth the risk I think Boss, otherwise we've got the best past of 2 days walking ahead of us."

"That's what I was thinking," said Jim, "the others are depending on us and one way or another we need to get some assistance. Preferably without any help from the local authorities but we can't just leave the guys there for another 3 days."

"If we get caught by the local Police do you think we'll be arrested?" asked Nick.

"No sure," said Jim, "I assume so. "Guess we need to try and avoid it, if we get detained I assume it will be embarrassing to the British Government and it'll probably put us out of action for a good bit."

"I suppose if we do get arrested we'll need to come clean about the others, we can't just leave them?" said Nick.

"No you are right" said Jim, "I think planning ahead if we are arrested we just say were are British Soldiers, name rank number and were on a mission to Argentina when we ran into bad weather and were accidentally dropped off by helicopter in Chile. We would have to give them something, so if we say that and stick to it, giving no other details. I can't think of anything else to do, what about you?"

"No Boss, I agree not saying anything isn't really an option. Besides which it is essentially true," said Nick.

"Always good to tell the truth, Nick, even if it is filtered a bit" said Jim with a laugh.

They made steady progress round the Bay and by first light were moving in a general Northerly direction. Looking north-west they could see the northern coastline of the bay. According to their map the track followed the coastline.

"Fucking long way Boss," said Nick.

"Yep, I was dreaming of some hot tea and a bacon sandwich," said Jim.

"Well I've saved a snickers bar, so that will have to do" he continued. He took it out of his pocket and using his knife cut it into 2 offering Nick half.

"Thanks," said Nick. "I'm down to my last packet of biscuits maybe we can eat those for lunch."

"Can't wait," said Jim.

The wind was blowing across the bay from the south west and it was quite cold, probably a few degrees above freezing, there were heavy shower clouds above although for the time being at least it was dry.

"Filthy climate," said Jim. "Even wetter and colder than at home, must be a bit like Scotland," he added with a smile, knowing it would make Nick bite.

"Careful boss," said Nick, "I don't even want this godforsaken place mentioned in the same sentence."

They continued walking and it got progressively lighter. By 1000hrs they hadn't seen anyone but had made reasonable progress with the sea on their left quite close to the track. They were alerted by a noise of a vehicle coming from behind.

"Looks like a pickup truck," said Nick.

"Yep, reckon this is it," said Jim. "Nothing much to lose, so let's see if we can get a lift."

They stayed at the side of the road so as not to look too desperate but waved their arms and stuck out their thumbs. The beaten up pickup ground to a halt. It was heavily laden with large logs, stacked in a pyramid in the back, there was a rope tied over the back. It all looked quite precarious but hey at least they had the possibility of a ride.

There were 3 men in the cab already. Fairly scruffy and unshaven, wearing lumberjack type shirts. They were looking at Nick and Jim somewhat curiously although their manner was quite friendly; the driver said something in Spanish which Jim didn't understand. Jim smiled and said "Porvenir," showing the driver the map.

The driver grinned and nodded and pointed to the back of the truck.

"Grassy ass," said Nick, remembering the list of key Spanish words they had all been issued with at the start of the Op.

The two weary soldiers climbed into the back of the truck; there was a small gap between the cab and the pyramid of logs. The truck pulled away. The small gap was a mixed blessing; it afforded some protection from the elements, although as the truck moved along the bumpy track the pyramid of logs seemed to lurch forwards towards the cab.

"Survived the helicopter only to get crushed to death by the logs," cracked Nick. It was noisy and windy and he shouted in Jim's ear.

Jim smiled; there was an element of truth in this as he felt the pressure of the logs as the truck went over a large bump.

Jim shouted back, "better than walking, reckon at this rate we'll be in Porvenir in about 2 hours, what do you think?"

"Assuming we don't pile in, you are probably right," said Nick.

It was pretty cold and they held on grimly but definitely a whole lot quicker and after about 2 hours the truck pulled up at a junction in the track. Jim and Nick climbed down and tried to get the stiffness from their limbs. They went across to the driver and thanked him, shaking his hand.

He pointed up the track and said a few words in Spanish, the soldiers picked up that he was pointing towards Porvenir.

"Teléfono," said Nick. The driver looked quizzically at him. Jim made out he was picking up a telephone handset and held it to his ear.

"Si," said the driver giving them the thumbs up. He went into a detailed explanation. Neither Jim nor Nick could understand but it seemed like he was explaining the location. They picked up the word radio and without being certain it seemed like he was telling them there was a radio phone located on the track.

"Reckon we can do our best to sort this out," said Jim. They bid farewell to the driver and his crew and as the truck moved off they started walking up the track towards Porvenir.

"This is going to be a bit tricky," said Jim.

"I know boss, I hope we get to the phone before we get arrested."

"Just go in and tough it out," said Jim.

"Let's try and find the phone first, then if we are still able we'll find somewhere to hole up."

As they approached Porvenir they realised it was not exactly a buzzing metropolis, it seemed like a random collection of wooden huts with verandas and boardwalks. The design of which seemed a little like something from a Clint Eastwood western. The only difference was that as far as Jim could remember it was always hot and sweaty in these particular westerns but that was an element of detail missing in this situation. It was fucking freezing.

There were no proper roads, just a muddy track with a few pot holes. There was not much traffic just a few beaten up 4 wheel drives parked on the side of the road. In fact far from attracting unwelcome attention the few people they saw seemed to take no notice.

Biting the bullet they approach an elderly man who was about to climb into his pickup.

He looked the soldiers up and down, and gave Jim a knowing grin.

"Inglés?"

Jim decided not to reply directly pretending not to understand.

He smiled and said "Teléfono," thinking great we had that list of key words, about the one think that has gone to plan.

"Si," said the Chilean, pointing up the road towards a wood shack, in the near distance Jim could see a small radio mast at the back with some supporting wires.

"Gracias," said Jim.

He and Nick moved rapidly towards the radio shack, not wishing to attract any further attention.

"Excellent, looks to be open," said Jim. They banged on the door and waited, at the bottom of the wooded steps. The door was opened by a middle aged man. He looked down curiously at the filthy, unshaven pair; despite the civilian jackets they were wearing combat trousers and military boots.

Jim said hullo and asked if the man if he spoke English. He shook his head but held up his hand indicating they should wait. He called out in Spanish to a younger man inside, he came to the door. The newcomer also looked at the soldiers and seemed a little perplexed. However he explained that he could understand some English and how could they help?

"Looking good," said Jim to Nick.

Without offering any explanation of how they came to be there Jim simply explained that they would like to make a telephone call. He pulled a $10 note from his pocket and gave it to the man. The older of the two men took the money and Nick and Jim were invited into the hut. Jim pulled his notebook and found the emergency number of the British Consul; this had been supplied before they had left Hereford. He wrote down the number for the operator who gave Jim a handset. The operator dialled the number and Jim could hear the phone ringing.

"Glory be," thought Jim as it the ringing stopped and it was answered.

"Hullo, William Sims speaking," said the English voice at the other end, no sign of any accent.

"You probably won't know me Sir," said Jim. He continued, "I'm a Captain in the British Army and the commander of an 8 man patrol currently in Chile. We need some assistance."

Jim heard a sharp intake of breath at the other end. No further comment so he continued.

"We are out of rations and need a resupply. What we really need from you is some assistance to help us locate a team from the British Army who have been sent to collect us."

"What the hell are you doing in Chile?" asked a stunned Mr Sims.

"Not really something we can discuss over the phone," said Jim.

"The only thing you can realistically do is to surrender yourselves to the Chilean Authorities. In fact you really must do this immediately. I urge you to do this he continued."

"Sounds a little panicky," thought Jim who perhaps unjustly in the circumstances found it hard to understand why the Consul should be so bothered.

"We want to avoid that if at all possible said Jim," who now on top of feeling a bit tired and hungry was starting to get irritated with the man.

"If nothing else can you please get a message to the British Authorities?" Asked Jim.

"My final word on this matter is that you immediately surrender yourselves to the Chilean Authorities." Mr Sims sounded quite angry. He put the phone down.

"Sounds like that went well, Boss," said Nick managing to grin despite the disappointment.

"Yep reckon I might have handled it a bit better," said Jim. "That's blown it. He actually sounded like he was shitting himself. Can't think why, I mean presumably he's in the warm and dry and it's not as though we actually asked for anything except him to help get a message to our people."

"What next?" Asked Nick.

"Let's get out of here, before we attract any unwelcome attention. Mind you we really need somewhere to hole up whilst we plan what to do next." Jim looked in the direction of the younger of the two radio operators. The latter looked up and smiled obligingly.

"We need somewhere to stay, do you know anywhere nearby?" Asked Jim.

"Yes just down the street, the house on the corner, this side of the road. Paco takes in guests he may be able to accommodate you."

"Brilliant," said Jim. "Let's give it a try."

With that the two soldiers shook hand with the radio operators, thanked them for their assistance and moved off.

Moving quickly up the street they banged on the glass paned door of a rather shabby single storey wooden building. It had a wooden cladding and badly needed repainting.

The door was answered by a middle aged man; he looked the 2 soldiers up and down and smiled inquisitively at them.

"Paco?" asked Jim.

The man nodded.

We need a room said Jim.

Jim could see he didn't understand and Nick pointed at the sign "habitación en alquiler."

Paco nodded, and despite their filthy and unshaven appearance they were invited in and shown along a narrow corridor into a small room with 2 single beds.

En route, he pointed to a small bathroom along the corridor.

Everything looked like it had seen better days, but it seemed quiet war and dry. They were off the street and would they hoped be able to plan they next move.

"Luxury, boss" said Nick touching the bed.

He looked at Jim. Jim nodded.

"This is great Paco, gracias. We will stay tonight"

Not really sure how much the room cost for the night Jim though a reasonably generous contribution is US $ might seal the deal and also maybe help to maintain Paco's full cooperation and even silence. He pulled out a $20 bill and handed it to Paco.

Paco's face lit up and he quickly put the bill into his pocket.

He pointed to his small kitchen and then his watch indicating some food would be available in about 1 hour.

"Just gets better and better boss, I like the sound of that." Nick was actually smiling.

They shut the door and sat on their beds. Just being out of the wind felt great, the ends of some of Jim's fingers were chapped and split and he could feel his face glow in the relative warmth of the room. They decided to get cleaned up, well rather a hands and face wash as no one had any razors or clean kit. Sleep was an inviting prospect but they needed to think first then get something to eat.

"I reckon we need some civvy kit if we are to move around and avoid too much attention," said Nick.

"Good idea," said Jim.

"After we get some food," I'll investigate whether there is anything we can buy. I've still got US $100," added Nick.

"I'm down to $70 after the phone call and the room."

"If we can get some civvies we might have another go on the phone, have a bash at calling Hereford," said Jim.

"Nothing much else we can do, no point in calling the other wanker again," confirmed Nick.

"I was thinking we could maybe hire some transport and collect the rest of the boys, although the problem will be where to move them to. On your shopping trip see if there is anywhere we can buy some food and we could take that to them. Maybe even move them a bit nearer," added Jim.

There was a knock on the door and Paco indicated they should follow him into the kitchen. They sat round a small formica table and waited whilst he cut bread and handed them each a bowl of lambs neck stew. There was plenty of bone and not too much meat but it was topped up with carrot and potatoes and the last decent cooked food had been the steak on the Invincible just before they had flown out. It was washed down with some black tea.

Wiping the dishes clean with a piece of bread, their host was watching a small wall mounted black and white TV. It was showing pictures of the Falklands conflict. Paco laughed and pointed to Nick and Jim and then back to the TV. Jim smiled back and put his finger to his mouth indicating quiet. Paco just nodded. He hoped that Paco wasn't about to rush off to the local Police Station. It seemed more likely that he would have already done so, pocketed the cash and not bothered about giving them food.

"Right boss, time to go shopping," said Nick.

"Best of luck, try not to get arrested," he managed to joke. Well at least it was intended as a joke.

They had agreed that only Nick would go it being slightly less obtrusive, Jim would remain in the room. At least it would give him some time to think. He wondered how the rest of the boys were fairing; he was feeling more than a little guilty about having been fed and in relatively warm dry place. They were exposed to the elements, out of rations and stuck in the middle over nowhere maybe about 120km away.

Jim lay on the bed, what next? Whilst his and Nick's personal fortunes had picked up a little, they were still in the shit, especially if they were to be arrested. Probably nothing terrible would happen but it would probably be an embarrassment to the British Government to say the least. He didn't know how to contact Rod and his team or even if they were in the area. The only thing would be to go back to the radio shack and see if were possible to call Hereford direct and speak to the duty officer.

He looked out of the window onto the street; it was starting to get dark. He looked at his watch. Nick had been gone for about 30 minutes. "Shit, I wonder if he's got a problem," Jim pondered. Just then he heard the front door open and a minute later Nick appeared carrying 2 bags.

"Surprisingly no one seemed to take any notice of my uniform or my accent," he said.

"I found a general store, pretty limited choice but I bought soap, razor, a lumberjack shirts and a pair of jeans each."

"Nice one," said Jim. "Shirt looks good, what the fuck size are these jeans?"

Jim held up the jeans against his chest they still touched the floor. This was quite an achievement as he was well over 6 feet tall.

"Reckon I could get 2 of me in them," he added. Slim at the best of times Jim would have to confess to having lost a few pounds over the past couple of weeks.

"Sorry boss, like I said limited choice and it was quite difficult to make them understand what I wanted."

"OK Nick sorry, I know you did your best. I'll ask Paco for some string to help keep them up," he grinned. "At least they are big enough."

"Reckon the shirts, jeans with our Cotswold camping coats on top might make it a bit less obvious we don't belong here, especially if we go out after dark." Nick added.

"Well let's give it a try, I want to check out the radio phone and maybe we can take a look round. Did you see anywhere to buy rations?"

"Same place boss, seems like they sell pretty much everything. Sort of like a general store in a western."

"Got it," said Jim. "Also need to check out whether we can get a vehicle of any sort in the event we need to resupply the boys."

Ten minutes later the two men moved onto the boardwalk. It was completely dark as they moved back towards the radio shed. Unfortunately it was shut. They would need to try later. They decided to walk around a little, as they had both been taught time spent in reconnaissance was seldom wasted.

A cold wind blew down the street, sleet in the air. Not much to see, Nick showed Jim the General Store which was also shut. They moved round the corner and a 4 by 4 was parked on the side of the road, outside what looked to be a restaurant, small tables with red and white check tablecloths. Perhaps this was too grand a word, at least somewhere to eat. It was brightly lit and there were no curtains. Inside 3 men sat at a table. Jim instantly recognised Rod and his 2 colleagues Charlie and Steve.

Chapter 16

Pickup

Jim and Nick waived through the glass window trying to attract some attention. In the end Jim said "Bollocks, let's just go in."

Rod and his 2 colleagues looked startled and stared at Jim and Nick with disbelief, "Jim, we had pretty much given up on you. We've been looking for you for days."

"Nice gear, Boss." added Steve with a warm smile.

Jim was still fundamentally filthy he and Nick had attempted to scrub up but it hadn't worked too well. He was wearing jeans that were about 4 sizes too big and his beloved Cotswold camping coat which was looking pretty tacky by this stage.

"Funny but we have been looking for you too," Jim managed to smile back.

Realizing they were attracting some strange looks from the owner Rod quickly handed Jim the keys to the 4X4 and told him to wait in the car whilst they paid up and made a rapid exit.

"We can catch up in the car in 5 minutes," he said.

5 minutes later and they were en route back to Paco's guest house which was just around the corner. Jim and Nick quickly collected their gear, which didn't amount to much. Paco merely raised an eyebrow when they said

goodbye, he smiled warmly as they shook hands and thanked him for his hospitality.

A further 5 minutes and they were outside of the town and in some disused farm buildings that Rod had taken over as a safe house.

Rod quickly explained that Steve and Charlie had been to the RV at last light every day for the past 4 days. He said that they had also chartered a light aircraft and stencilled 'Jim' under the wings and flown daily over the country on the Chilean side of the border. Apparently there were a large number of Argentinian troops still looking for Jim's patrol, their military having been alerted following the discovery of the wreckage of the Sea King helicopter.

Jim briefly explained the events of the previous 5 days since the aborted insertion. He showed Rod the map and where the rest of the patrol was holed up.

"This is where we think the RV is, there is a bridge over the river, just here." Jim explained.

Charlie pulled out a more up to date map, "we managed to obtain this one locally when we arrived," he added.

Continuing he said, "It's hard to tell from your map, but we have opened the RV here." His pencil pointed to an area on the road further to the east of Jim's position.

"Looks like we may have missed each other by a few kilometres," said Jim.

"Your map is pretty fucked up, Boss," said Steve.

"Anyway we can discuss the fine detail of what went wrong later, how are we going to collect the rest of the boys?" asked Jim.

"We have 2 4X4 vehicles, Steve and Charlie will drive taking you and Nick as guides. Rod explained.

"Sounds good, how soon can we start?" asked Jim.

"Good to go now Boss," said Steve. "It'll take around 2 hours to get there. So allowing for 15 minutes locating the team and get the team all loaded up about 4 and a half hour round trip."

"Can we get some food ready for them when we get back, we were all out of rations yesterday and they'll be seriously hungry," said Jim.

"All sorted, went shopping earlier Boss, so we'll do tea and bacon sandwiches all round," added Charlie.

"Excellent," said Jim, "let's go then."

The journey in the 4X4 was slow but uneventful with Jim struggling to stay awake. There was light snow falling but nothing that serious. About 2 hours later they stopped at the bridge that Jim believed to be the RV. Jim and Nick went off to find their patrol.

The snow had stopped and the moon was out which helped light up the way as they moved towards the lie up position. As they moved near Nick whistled softly, reassuringly he got a whistled response.

Jim heard a low voice say "Nick and the Boss are back," followed by the sounds of zips and rustling sleeping bags.

"We've found Rod, and Charlie and Steve are waiting on the track to pick us up," said Nick.

"Bloody wonderful, well done boys," said Ed.

He slapped Jim on the back, whilst Rob had Nick in a bear hug.

"How long before you are ready to get out of here?" asked Jim. We can fill you in on the details on the way back.

"About 2 minutes," laughed Ed.

Everyone was scrambling to push sleeping bags and any spare layers of clothing into their Bergen.

10 minutes later and they were back in the waiting vehicles and heading to the safe house.

Two hours later and they were unpacking their kit. There was a barn area, some running water and what looked in the darkness to be a patio with a built in BBQ. Rod had organised the tea and there were hot bacon sandwiches.

Jim thought that it was one of the nicest things he had ever eaten, it barely touched the sides.

The boys were catching up with Charlie and Steve, he could hear Mike saying, "So where the fuck were you, whilst we have been starving?" in the background.

"I don't want to spoil the party but there is some really bad news Jim," said Rod.

Jim looked at Rod; it was difficult to feel much emotion given the events of the past few weeks. "Go on," he said.

"We lost 18 men from G and D Squadrons when a Sea King ditched into the sea, it would have been 19 May, 2 days after your insertion. I've got the names of those killed, it's a real blow for the Regiment." Rod looked at Jim.

"That's terrible; I was only talking to Paul the afternoon before we took off. He said he had just got back to Hereford after a few months away and then left to join the fleet immediately without managing to say hullo and goodbye to his wife and young son."

"I'm afraid he was one of the ones killed," said Rod.

"Shocker," said Jim. He felt more than a little guilty. Here they all were, alive and well. Apart from a few scary moments the worst thing that had happened was that they a got a bit cold and hungry.

"Best tell the others," he said to Rod.

The following morning the patrol were in somber mood. Rod and Charlie had disappeared for a few hours no explanation had been given and Jim knew better than to ask.

Eventually when they reappeared Rod called Jim and his team together.

Rod sipped his tea and went on.

"It seems that things are getting a bit hot to handle, there has been a lot of interest in your ditched helicopter and the word is out that 2 English soldiers were seen in town yesterday. We need to move you away from here."

"Where to?" Asked Jim.

"Santiago, to a safe house. From there we can assess our options."

"We were thinking we might be useful here," said Jim.

"Possibly get close to the border and view the ground to Rio Grande."

"Too risky at the moment, we definitely don't want to upset the Chileans, we are being assisted by their Air Force and we really need them onside." Rod continued.

"We may well bring you back in due course but for the time being this is our only option. There are two stages, firstly we move by light aircraft to Punta Arenas and then onto a different aircraft to Santiago. It's a long trip and we refuel at Puerto Montt, it's about halfway.

"Ok," said Jim, "so when do we leave?"

"About 20 minutes," said Rod with a grin.

"By the way we need you all to change into civvies, Charlie has been shopping."

"I hope he knows my size better that Nick," said Jim.

2 hours later they had transferred from one light aircraft to a slightly larger one with twin engines at an airstrip near to Punta Arenas.

"Just enough room for all of us and our kit, Boss," said Ed.

They were introduced to their Chilean Air Force pilot Juan.

Everything started well, the weather was freezing cold but fairly bright, a brisk wind blew in the odd snow flurry.

Apart from it growing increasingly cold the first 20 minutes passed without event as their plane worked its way northwards.

Jim looked down between the heavy clouds, he could see the coastline, nothing below but mountains covered in snow and glaciers going into the sea. Very bleak and inhospitable, not much chance to survive down there he thought.

It was noisy in the plane so very little opportunity to talk. He looked at Ed and pointed below. Ed nodded as if to understand that would not be a good place to land.

Another 10 minutes and it was freezing, the ski type jackets they had been given by Charlie were fairly warm but with a t-shirt underneath and even with the buttons fully done up Jim was feeling the cold. He looked around others had buttoned up their jackets fully and were clearly feeling the same.

Suddenly there was a load buzzing which Jim took to be some kind of alarm. It went on intermittently for the next hour. Rod who was in the front passed the message back that it was the stall warning indicator going off because it had iced up.

Jim thought, "Fucking great, more drama" he looked around trying to find some comfort in the somewhat pale faces around him. Finding none he tried to look out of the window, this had frosted over completely so the only thing to do was sit tight and assume everything was going to plan. "No sign of panic up front," he thought so he supposed must be normal for the alarm to go off in the current conditions.

As far as Jim was aware the plan was still making progress northwards. Eventually things started to warm up and the nonsense with the stall warning alarm stopped. Rod passed another message back. They were approaching Puerto Montt but there was a little problem. The pilot was unable to fully control the plane for landing as a result of the earlier icing conditions. Juan would be putting the plane into a shallow dive, the idea being to try and crack the ice off the controls so they could land and refuel.

As the latest message went round Jim tried to look phlegmatic and studied the faces around him, no one said much, after their recent helicopter ride it seemed situation normal.

As the plane dived you could hear the ice cracking as it broke up and came away from the plane.

Everyone sat expressionless just listening to the cracking ice.

Jim felt a surge of relief as the plane pulled out of the dive, he gave the thumbs up to Ed who grinned and made out as though he was wiping his brow.

5 minutes later and they landed at Puerto Montt. Jim noted that after they had landed safely Juan crossed himself and mopped his brow. Good man he thought, didn't realise it was quite so close he just let us think that things were fairly routine. The drill was for them to stay on-board whilst the refuel was taking place. Jim looked outside, the freezing conditions they had encountered further south had passed, it was drizzling and the sky was overcast.

As the plane flew further north the weather became more benign. It was dark before they had landed at Santiago and stars were bright in the sky. As soon as the plane landed they were guided into 2 waiting cars. Rod told them there equipment would be delivered separately. 30 minutes later they arrived at house with a walled garden in what looked to be a quiet suburb. There were security gates and then a small drive to a large bungalow surrounded by Eucalyptus trees.

"Great pad," said Ed. "This looks pretty comfortable."

During the ensuing 8 days they were on standby to fly south so they dried out and prepared their equipment. There were takeaway meals delivered 3 times a day and books, playing cards and chess. They were not allowed out of the grounds but could venture into the garden. The days were clear and fairly warm it felt good to feel the sun.

In the meantime Jim was asked to write a detailed patrol report covering the period from the take-off on Invincible to the pick-up in Porvenir. In particular to describe the events at the time Jim had decided to abort the initial drop off. When he completed his account it was taken away by Rod.

After writing the report Jim felt depressed and increasingly bad about the whole business; here they were safe warm and well fed. Nothing had been blown up, not a shot fired in anger. A valuable Sea King had been lost and the aircrew had risked their necks trying to get them to the target. Many of their mates in the task force had clearly not fared so well. He Jim had taken the decision to abort and maybe that had saved them, he would never know but it sure as hell didn't stop him feeling bad. In fact all the time there was an increasing sense of foreboding, like he had done something so dreadfully wrong, so much so that it made him feel quite sick and although hungry he never seemed to have much of an appetite.

The next 8 days passed uneventfully. Boredom had set in; they received regular reports of the war through the embassy and whilst no one said anything Jim could tell that like him they all felt like spare pricks, stuck in Santiago whilst the action took place in the South Atlantic.

There was talk from Rod of various options to re-deploy Jim and his team. One was to move down the river to Rio Grande in small boats. None of these options materialised and they remained on standby.

They were all quite shocked to learn that Juan has disappeared on his flight back to Punta Arena, during the second leg from Peurto Montt. Rod had told him that there had been an ice storm and a mayday signal but no trace could be found of Juan's plane. Jim recalled the harsh coastline and the glaciers going into the sea. Maybe the stall warning was a gypsies warning thought Jim. You never know when your number is up and that was the final chance. So far Jim considered, they had in many ways been lucky, or at least that's the way it should have felt, although personally it just made him feel worst.

Finally on the 8th morning Rod came in early and announced they were to be sent back to the UK and needed to be ready to move in 1 hour to be taken to the airport. They would fly on a commercial flight, first from Santiago to Sao Paulo and then onto Lisbon and finally London. At no stage would they leave the aircraft. Rod handed round the passports which had been recovered from Hereford.

"You'll be allocated separate seats and on the journey back act like individuals try to avoid any discussions with passengers about your visit to Chile is that understood?"

Pack up your baggage and weapons and leave them in the hallway. It will all follow you back to Hereford.

They nodded and moved off to pack up their kit.

30 minutes later and they were moving through the security gates and heading to the airport.

Looking out of the car window Jim's final memory of Santiago was to be of a body in a pool of blood lying at the side of the road. There had been some sort of accident, he presumed the man to be dead, the body looked kind of battered, but there was no way of knowing as they sped off. People were just walking round the man's body just going about their daily business as though it was a common occurrence.

Chapter 17

Epilogue 30 years later

The sun was setting and Jim realised how cold he felt. Maybe not because the temperature was low but he just started to shiver, there were goose pimples on his bare arms. He sipped his beer listening to the stream of questions. He felt like had never been subjected to such an in depth interview and never before had he spoken in any depth of the events 30 years earlier.

They had gone through the whole business about the operation, at least as best as he could remember, from the training through to the pickup in Chile. The interviewer even wanted to know about Jim's background. Not wishing to be evasive Jim did his best but kept the details sketchy and brief, he had grown up on dairy farm, gone to university, master's degree mathematics, signed up practically on a whim after 4 pints one evening with the Army University Liaison Officer, passed out of a graduate entry course at Sandhurst, joined his infantry unit, passed SAS selection a year later, in fact looking back had led quite a charmed life really. In giving details like this he felt uncomfortable, in many ways he wondered why he had agreed to the request in the first place. Over the years he had been contacted several times asking if he wanted to give his account of events on the helicopter but he had always declined. Resurrecting the past had too many unpleasant memories, on reflection maybe more like lots of pleasant ones spoiled by the wrong ending. It had all gone so wrong on his return, picking up the pieces was tough at first, and he missed the excitement and camaraderie. For many years he felt like he needed anonymity and had avoided reunions and only ever kept in touch with a few close knit friends from the old days.

"When you got back to UK, what happened?" asked the interviewer.

"There was a board of inquiry to determine what had gone wrong on the operation. I suppose it was inevitable, such high profile operation, heavy political overtones, we write off a Sea King, risk the crew getting us there, wind up in Chile, the whole thing must have been pretty embarrassing for the British Authorities," said Jim.

"What did you think about it?" asked the interviewer.

"At the time I suppose I was feeling fairly angry maybe that was a layer of emotion to disguise the personal guilt and failure. I felt like we had all been put into a fairly untenable situation. Wrong to say this I suppose, given the 'Who Dares Wins' ethos but being from a mathematical background the probability of success must have been ridiculously low. We lacked intelligence about the target area and there were no sufficiently detailed maps available. In time we could have gained this information but in my opinion the search and destroy part of the mission was unlikely to succeed. The method of insertion seemed pretty much guaranteed to attract unwelcome attention before we even landed. I think a mission into Argentina from across the border would have given us the opportunity to fill in many of the missing gaps so that we could work out a better plan to strike at the enemy."

Jim paused, sipped some more beer and continued. "Of course looking back we were at war and many would argue that such risks needed to be taken, perhaps if only to demonstrate our political will. As I said we needed time and the reality of the situation was that the Task Force needed something done about the Exocet threat urgently." Jim paused for more beer.

"So how do you feel about the business now?" asked the interviewer.

"I'm still haunted by my decision to abort the first drop off. The intention was to move to a secondary drop off point and continue the mission but as you know this was not possible because of the weather and we ended up quite a long way into Chile, the rest is just history."

"Why does it haunt you still?"

"From a rational perspective I suppose I did the right thing, at least by the book, no patrol commander wants to lead his men directly into a possible compromise. In this situation there was understandably tremendous pressure. The weight of expectation, the extraordinary lengths to which so many had gone to get us there, being prepared to write off a helicopter and the aircrew, it felt somehow like I had transgressed and come what may we should have taken the risk. It's difficult, you are in a no win situation but it doesn't stop you feeling bad." Jim swished the remains of his beer round the bottom of the glass.

"At the end of the day you emerged with your patrol intact and I don't suppose they would have thanked you if you had led them directly into an Argentinian ambush," said the interviewer.

"Difficult," said Jim, "some may have seen it as an opportunity, a moment of destiny perhaps? At least afterwards," he managed to smile. "At least I've been lucky to have seen my kids grow up."

"So what happened at the board of enquiry?" asked the interviewer.

"The bottom line conclusion was that no direct blame could be apportioned but there may have been errors of judgement made in extremely difficult operational circumstances."

"So you didn't need to leave the SAS or mess up your career or anything like that?"

"No not at all, I was not asked to leave the SAS or the Army, however I finished my military career pretty much there and then; I left of my own volition. As I've said I felt down about the business and quite angry. I'm sure I wasn't particularly compromising at the time. After the Board of Enquiry I made up my mind rightly or wrongly that I didn't want to be remembered as the man that had pulled the plug on the mission. Also it didn't feel good that we had gone so far and achieved nothing, when many of our comrades would not be coming back." Jim went on, "so I told the new CO that I would leave but first I wanted to be allowed to return to the rest of the Squadron until the war was over, and then I would go. After it was over I would resign and leave the Army."

"What happened then?" Asked the interviewer.

"By this stage the war was practically over, I didn't get the chance to re-join the Squadron, in fact I resigned and we were done. I never wore a uniform or picked up an Armalite or 9mm Browning again, it really was the last patrol for me."

"What do you think about the people that planned the mission and ordered you to go?" the interviewer drained his glass.

"At the time I thought they were smoking something but looking back I can see the tremendous pressure everyone was under so I suppose they were only doing their jobs. I don't think in their hearts they could have thought there was too much chance of success for either my patrol or perhaps even less for the rest of the Squadron to land at Rio Grande. Still it just shows the level of desperation to have even considered such options."

"How do you feel about your own service now, would you do it again if you had the chance?" asked the interviewer reaching for another beer.

Jim pulled the ring on his beer, the gas exhaled slowly with a hiss. He gulped the cold beer directly from the tin.

"I suppose I would, it's the most fantastic feeling being in the Regiment, it stays with you forever, the excitement of belonging and working with such a team. Sometimes fate takes a turn for the worst, like on this occasion, it's almost like the powers that be believe you can walk on water. So survival depends to some extent on your luck, I suppose as I mentioned earlier there can be a high price to be paid for belonging to the team and this should never be forgotten."

"For me it didn't have a happy ending. Strange given some of the events I have described. People might actually reasonably think we were very lucky, the real problem for me was and still is, feeling like you have to let it all go, no longer being accepted as part of it and even worst carry on living with the legacy of guilt, which sadly, no matter how much beer you drink never completely goes away."

"Thanks for your time." The interviewer concluded the interview.

Appendix
Weapons

C4 explosives approx. 4lb per man and 4 timing devices,

Silenced weapon – Welrod 'assassins weapon' http://en.wikipedia.org/wiki/Welrod 73db

M16 Armalite 5.56mm - every man, 120 rounds

Browning 9mm pistol - every man 30 rounds

Equipment

SAS Bergen and Belt kit

Cam nets

Sleeping bag – either army issue or hollow fill (useless)

1 man tents (commercial design, no poles)

Rations 4 days min (in the event not enough)

Waterproof coat – commercial design

Satellite communications device and spare battery

Knife

Silva compass

Binos

Timeline

Date 1982 (estimated)	Event	Comments
Sun 4 April	OC briefing	B Squadron Bradbury Lines Hereford
4 April – 7 May	Squadron training	Patrol skills, communications, range work, explosives, night marches, C130 aircraft drills, parachuting, mock 'attacks' on UK airfields
7 May	Selection of personnel for Reconnaissance patrols	Estimated time
9 May	Initial briefing for Reconnaissance patrols	Estimated time, 2 targets Rio Gallegos 9 Troop and Rio Grande 6 Troop
11 May	Merge patrols	Rio Gallegos only target, from pure reconnaissance to fighting patrol
13 May	Patrol briefing	Director of Special Forces
14 May	Depart Hereford	
15 May	Ascension Island	
16 May	Parachute into Fort Austin and	Night on Hermes

	moved to HMS Hermes	
17 May	Move to Invincible, meet aircrew of Sea King and plan insertion	HMS Invincible
17 -18 May	Insertion	Sea King to mainland
18 May	Compromise at drop off	Head for back up drop off
18 May	Drop off in Chile	Unable to make back up drop off, combination of radar detection and very poor visibility
18 May	Walk Eastwards until first light	3-4 hours until first light. Very wet, cold rain turning to snow. Thick lying snow by morning
18 May	Lie up during day. Determine position.	Vic becomes sick, gets dosed up, radio back to Hereford, explain situation.
19 May	Lie up in day. Hereford believes patrol has been captured, asked to authenticate.	Vic feeling slightly better that evening. Walk eastwards that night. Work out rough position determine that still maybe 10 km

		short of the border and 35 Km from Rio Grande.
20 May	Discuss position within patrol. Still short of the border, each man approximately 1-2 days rations left.	Vic feeling better. Weather wet cold. Some snow.
21 May	Inform Hereford will need a resupply. Advised to make way back to an agreed RV	Plan to be collected by Maj Rod and team
21-22 May	March about 15 km to locate RV. No radio, all comms dead.	RV planned to be open for 1 hour after dark
22 May	No one at RV	
23 May	No one at RV	
24 May	No one at RV	
25 May	No one at RV	Can't recall whether it was 3 days or 4, waiting
26 May	Patrol Jim and Nick seek assistance head down main coastal road towards Porvenir. Remainder wait at ERV	Leave rifles and equipment, keep 9mm pistol. Plan to find a phone and seek assistance from British Consul
26 May	Walk then pick up lift on truck carrying logs	Walk/Hitch lift to Porvenir, about 50 miles

	along coastal road	
26 May	Find radio phone in shack and call British Consul	Advised to give ourselves up to Chilean authorities, Consul not a happy bunny.
26 May	Jim and Nick find accommodation (and food!)	Nick buys civilian clothes, jeans and jumper.
26 May	Go for walk after dark in new civvies and quite by chance find Rod and team in a local eating house	Restaurant is probably too posh a word
26-27 May	Return to ERV locate and pick up patrol and equipment	Great relief in patrol, taken to safe house (barn)
27-29 May	Recovery at safe house	Now awaiting fresh orders and resupply, believed likely to be ordered back over the border to complete mission or at least undertake reconnaissance. Learn of SAS helicopter crash in South Atlantic, real shock in team as many good

		friends have been killed. Also learn that our Sea King was discovered in Chile, we understand "3,000" (according Rod) Argentinian troops scouring the border looking for SAS.
30 May	Taken to Punta Arenas, airfield and loaded with kit onto another light aircraft	Moved by light aircraft in civilian clothes. Believed necessary to be moved because of the high level of ground activity/interest and needed to remain covert
30 May	Flown Santiago	Flew northwards up west coast of Chile. Leg to Puerto Montt, very cold and significant icing, quite unpleasant experience. Pilot dives to break up ice and free up controls, crosses himself on landing. Refuel at Puerto Montt, Jim and

		patrol remains onboard.
30 May-7 Jun	Santiago	Second leg to Santiago nowhere near as dramatic. Moved directly to safe house in suburbs. Review options to fly south again. Learn that pilot who flew us north disappeared after a 'mayday' signal on flight back, leg Puerto Montt to Punta Arena.
8 Jun	Return UK	Told of plan to return to UK and within hours reunited with passport and on a civilian flight, refuel Sao Paulo and Lisbon.
8 Jun	Return Group HQ/Hereford	
9-10 Jun	Debrief Hereford	
14 Jun	Board of Enquiry	Held at Group HQ London

Printed in Poland
by Amazon Fulfillment
Poland Sp. z o.o., Wrocław